HEART OF RESCUE

A BIPOLAR AND PTSD SELF-HELP MEMOIR

JOHN TOWNS

Gray Area
Press

Heart of Rescue: A Bipolar and PTSD Self-Help Memoir

Copyright © 2020 John Kline

Cover Photo: Sunrise of hope through dark clouds over the Outer Banks of North Carolina

ISBN #13 978-0-578-74294-6 (Print)

ISBN #13 978-0-578-74295-3 (E-book)

Library of Congress Control Number: 2020917763

BIOGRAPHY & AUTOBIOGRAPHY / Personal Memoirs

SELF-HELP / Mood Disorders / Bipolar Disorder

Published by Gray Area Press, Wake Forest, North Carolina, USA

Note: Names and identifying characteristics have been changed to protect privacy. The following is not intended as medical advice.

Chapter Five Note: Goodwin FK, Jamison KR. *Manic-Depressive Illness*. New York: Oxford University Press; 1990.
https://www.psychiatrictimes.com/view/suicide-attempts-and-completions-patients-bipolar-disorder

For my wife who didn't want me to write this book because she thought it might bring back bad memories but slowly became its main supporter. She exemplifies how another person can make such a difference to someone with bipolar.

To all of us who need rescuing and all of us who rescue in so many different ways.

Brother Jay, who was always there.

Bernadette S. Simme, MSN, APRN, BC, who reviewed the manuscript with knowledge and compassion.

CONTENTS

PROLOGUE

THE SHOOTER WAS ON THE SECOND FLOOR NEAR THE top of the stairs. Oddly enough, the call came into the base as an "injury." When we rolled up in the ambulance to the dilapidated hotel, we were surprised to hear gunfire from inside. We went into the lobby and found two wounded people hiding behind a ratty old couch. The gunman was one flight up, evidently targeting everyone he could find. Wounded people flew or tumbled down the stairs with absolute terror on their faces. As my partner called for police backup, I rushed the first two victims to the ambulance. Both had been shot in the leg. The shooting continued, and I hurried back into the tiny lobby. People ran out from their rooms to escape. Many were shot at the top of the stairs. I glued myself against the lobby wall at the bottom of the stairs. Hopefully, I was out of the line of fire. I brushed against a picture that was on the wall, and it crashed to the floor. Did the shooter hear it? Did it give away my position? More panicked, wounded people ran down. As we hustled the rest of the victims to the rig and went back in, it occurred to me the bastard might now come down the steps to finish us off. The bedlam continued. Then the shooting finally stopped.

Our ambulance, designed for two patients, now held nine victims. It almost felt like a bizarre clown car, holding way more people than I thought possible. Six had leg wounds, one had an arm wound, one was shot in the back, and another was shot in the stomach. The first police cars were finally arriving, and it was time for us to go. As we pulled away from the scene, it was standing room only for most of my patients. Everyone was still conscious and glad to be out of the hotel from hell. On the way to the ER, the standing patients' noses were pressed against the wall of the speeding ambulance. I doubt they minded the ride.

It looked like a small-caliber weapon was used, probably a .22. We were lucky; all the victims survived that crazy night and would be able to go back to their families. My partner and I would too. You might think that the shooter was mentally ill, but that was not the case. The bastard turned out to be a very drunk long-term alcoholic with no hope and nothing to lose.

That incident occurred at a "flophouse" hotel where alcoholics, addicts, and the almost homeless lived a day-to-day existence. You could say that was a bad night in the tough area of the city where I worked as an Emergency Medical Technician, or EMT. I don't think the incident even made the news. That was an era when many said "Who cares if the destitute and homeless shoot each other?" Today mass shootings make the news frequently, and we seem to care more. Is it because shootings seem to affect more than the inner-city poor and forgotten?

What gave me the right, privilege, and responsibility—a guy who had been misdiagnosed with schizophrenia and then correctly diagnosed with bipolar disorder and PTSD with a history of psychosis and shock treatments—to try to save human lives? When I think about it, if I were a patient, would I be thrilled to know my rescuer had a history of mental illness?

Yet through all the chaos and heartbreak, I am most proud of my career in emergency medicine, which allowed me to make the most difference. How could it not? I became a crew chief on an ambulance in Elizabeth, New Jersey, about twelve miles from the Statue of Liberty. I worked in the part of town known as "The Port," the dangerous part of the city. I chose the graveyard shift because it got the largest share of emergency calls. There were some high points in the twenty-seven or so other jobs I had, but nothing was as fulfilling as ambulance and disaster work. Preservation of life ranks high on the human spectrum of life.

I managed to appreciate, enjoy, and in between serious mental setbacks, cram in a life of adventure, service, and downright fun. A life lived, not allowed to be short-changed by mental illness. What follows is a collection of separate stories of my life and how I learned to accept and manage bipolar ups and downs with PTSD to become more than a diagnosis and bucket of symptoms.

I've had over fifty years to get this stuff right and share it with you. Although not a cure, my experiences and practical tips may help to enhance or better your life. If you or someone you know has a mental illness, or for that matter finds things hard or seemingly impossible, my sincere wish for you is that this book will inspire and offer possibilities.

Are you diagnosed with a mental illness? Always in a state of anxiety or depression? Can't even think of getting out of bed? Can't get to sleep? Racing thoughts? Life doesn't offer much? Wonder what's the point? Suicide an option?

The list goes on and feels endless. I still wonder about these things. If you're lucky enough to get professional help and perhaps the right medications, the list can dwindle. Bipolar disorder can take you from euphoric highs of manias to the darkest depressions you will ever know. Normal times may be fleeting only to be replaced by a lifetime of frightening mood swings which leave you wondering if they will ever stop. Holding on to a relationship or a job will take incredible amounts of strength. I found a professional is essential to make possibilities reachable. Even then, problems may still come back. When we accept ourselves and our illness, we achieve something worthwhile. When we take responsibility for ourselves, that is the beginning of getting and staying well. I don't mean pull yourself up by your bootstraps; that's not possible. What I mean is to think about your situation and take conscious actions to understand your problems and work at realistic plans to solve them.

For a while, I was immersed in sadness, self-pity, defeat, depression, and madness, and was taking myself deathly seriously. Treatment and hard work helped minimize bad cycles and let me grab onto better times when I could squeeze out some "normalcy." I was able to have fun and engage in life!

It helps to do things that make you happy: watch a favorite movie, listen to music, eat a favorite treat, talk with family or friends, or take a walk. When we make our happiness, it breeds more fun and fulfillment. To be truly happy, or at least to be mostly satisfied with life, I learned to step away from myself and help someone else; this works for me every single time!

These thoughts I share with you are what happened to me and what is still happening. Some say I was lucky. Some that I made my own luck. Some of my experiences, failures, and successes may give you some useful coping ideas or strategies. I am not a doctor or counselor and do not intend the following to be medical advice. It is my sincere hope to you that you can see that all is not lost. You may not be able to cure yourself; that's not what rescue is. It is taking a bad situation and making it better. If it gives you ideas that ease your burden or even rescues you, then I am a fulfilled and happy guy.

1

THE BEGINNING

Can't Breathe Underwater

I WAS A SHY, THIN, INTROVERTED, AND QUIET adolescent starting high school. I was uncomfortable in my own skin and socially awkward. I slept my way through high school, earning the nickname of "instant sleep." I would put my head down on the desk and just go to sleep. My other nickname was "mister analytical" because when I was awake, I asked thoughtful questions. Thinking back, maybe the sleeping was the beginning of bipolar depression.

The depression lifted in my junior year when I trained to be a lifeguard and got a job at a large municipal pool outside the city. We always had six lifeguards on duty; four walkers and one on each of the elevated lifeguard stands near the deep-diving area. The kids were inner-city kids, bused to the pool. Most couldn't swim or thought they could but couldn't. Over two summers, I was able to save eleven children from drowning.

One day in particular stands out. I was on one of the elevated lifeguard stands known as sticks, where my responsibility was to watch the diving boards and keep swimmers from going past the ropes that delineated shallow water from the diving area. It was a typical hot day, and everyone was having fun, and most of the kids were even obeying the rules. I constantly checked the deep-diving area as well as the part of the pool that went from waist deep to fifteen feet. Being higher up on the stick, I had a good view of the swimmers and made mental notes of who was where and if they were still coming up for air. Everything was hunky-dory. I would occasionally look down past my feet to check the little patch of deep water under the stick. It's a blind spot unless you consciously lean forward and look down. This time, when I looked down, something wasn't as it was supposed to be. The bottom of the pool had wide black swimming lane lines, and one of the lines had something moving on it. It looked like a kind of undulating motion that appeared to be part of the line. It was the skinny arms and legs of a little black girl in a black bathing suit on the black line. She was almost impossible to see at the bottom of the pool, blending almost perfectly with the line. If I hadn't looked carefully, I would have missed her. I dove in after her and brought her up. She was scared and confused, but other than that she was fine.

Saving someone's life, especially a child's, is intensely satisfying. In my little suburban life, I had never done anything like that. It gave me pride and some confidence that I had never had before. It seemed impossible, but maybe John, the misfit, found something that fit. My experiences here planted the seed of something that would become a good part of my life and a good part of this book. I found my niche.

Someday you may have the opportunity to save someone from drowning. It's not like you see in Hollywood. You don't swim up to a panicked thrashing person, put your arm around their chest, and tow them in unless that victim is a small child. Here's what will probably happen. An adult will be so frightened and desperate to stay above water that he will grab on to you.

You become his island, and he climbs up you, pushing you below the surface. He may not be able to listen to anything you tell him to do. His grip may be impossible to escape. It's a death grip. You both sink. There are cases when a second rescuer tries to help, which results in three people locked together below the surface. It's simple to avoid this life or death struggle. All you have to do is before you enter the water, grab anything that floats. A large ball, a cooler, a large thermos, a life jacket, whatever is available. When you get to the drowning person, toss it to him, and he will grab it. Of course, before you started your rescue, you told someone to call 911. Now the person can float until the pros come. You both go home that day.

I Woke Up Dead

That's the only way I can describe how my "normal" life was lost in one night. The summer before college, I was on my motorcycle, coming home from my lifeguard job. Other than my helmet, all I had on was my bathing suit and sandals. No leathers for me! The driver of the oncoming car at the intersection didn't see me and made a left turn in to my path. I was doing about forty when I rammed into the side of her car and flew over her vehicle. For a split second, I saw the woman's startled face. The bike went careening into the middle of the intersection, and I landed near the curb. My bike was revved up with the throttle wide open, and I had to shut it down, or the engine would be ruined. I tried to get up from the street but found my right leg useless. My adrenaline must have been pumping because I was able to hop over to the bike and turn the key to shut down my mangled bike. It felt dreadful, like I was shooting my dying horse. My leg was broken, and I was severely scraped up, but there was no pain. A little too late for this dumbass to see why people wear leather clothing when riding. The other driver was at fault, and her insurance company paid for a new bike and a fashionable white hip-to-foot cast for my leg.

I ended up starting my freshman year five hundred miles from home with that white elephant. A big leg cast signed with well-wishes but a white elephant nonetheless. Other than scout camp with my older brother, I had never been away from home. Everything in my life was different at college: new state, new people, new routine, and new responsibilities. I felt so little, insignificant, and out of control at the university. It was all so overwhelming. The cast didn't help either. I went through freshmen orientation, which didn't orient me in the least. I knew my roommate, where the dining hall was, and the general directions of where my classes would be. As the first weeks went by, the cast was removed, and I was scheduled to take my first biology practical lab test. It would be a large part of my grade, so it was important. I don't know how, but I forgot about the test and promptly got behind in the course. Science was my main interest, so that was upsetting.

I hadn't made any friends yet, so I pledged a fraternity called "the Bucks," who considered themselves the pirates on campus. Not exactly a traditional Greek fraternity. I guess I was a rebel. The night I woke up dead, I had gone out with some of the brothers who were pledging me. We had some beers, and then I came back to the dorm to study and try to catch up. At that point in my limited college career, I was getting further and further behind in my studies. I was staying up late, hitting the books, when a guy knocked on the door. He said he was selling uppers and that they would help me study. Well, I certainly needed all the help I could get, so I bought some amyl nitrite. It came in a glass capsule, which was about an inch long wrapped lightly in gauzelike material. My benefactor at the door had instructed me to break the capsule between my fingers and then deeply inhale the fumes.

Being a drug virgin, the closest thing I had ever taken to that was Vic's VapoRub. My little experiment did more than clear my sinuses. It is also used medically to treat chest pains. Today we commonly call this gem of a substance "poppers." It is used as a sexual stimulant. It does have some side effects. It speeds up your heart. What it did for me was speed up my heart to the point I felt my pulse pounding in my chest and neck. Since I had been drinking, the effects were even stronger. I'm not sure of the sequence of events that led up to me finding myself in an off-campus club featuring loud music with huge walls all around with cartoon-like images flashing around in psychedelic patterns. It is thought that my future fraternity brothers brought me there as part of their hazing process. The later university investigation concluded that one of the "pirates" from the frat crew had laced my drink with LSD. Timothy Leary, here I come. The guys who I hoped would be my friends left me there with no way of getting back to campus. Pretty funny, right? The only problem was, with the combination of amyl nitrite, LSD, and beer, I was rapidly becoming psychotic. I was losing my mind. That was not the way it was supposed to be.

I must have been wandering the streets and found myself on the roof of a ten-story hotel. I went to the edge of the roof and marveled at all the twinkling lights and the line of illuminations on the horizon. I ran to the other side of the roof, this time even closer to the edge. I wanted to see if the lights were even better. I felt at one with them and wanted to join their glory. I don't know why I didn't jump. Like everything else that was happening to me, it could have gone any which way. I found myself in a long corridor of the hotel with a bright red carpet and doors to rooms on either side. I sat down against the wall and passed out. The next thing I remember was being loaded into the back of a police car. At some point, I woke up dead in the emergency room. I was restrained to a gurney, didn't know where I was, who I was, what happened, and why I was there. I couldn't think, reason, or talk. I had to be alive, but I was functionally a dead man. I wouldn't be the only person in this book who speed killed.

I don't know how long I was there before my mom flew down to take me home. I think I recognized her, but I'm not entirely sure. We got on the plane. Turns out, the doctors did not adequately sedate me for the flight. I don't know what I was doing, but they kicked the "crazy" person off the plane. I don't blame them; back to the hospital for another shot. I can't imagine what Mom must have been going through. Dad was currently in the hospital, and she had lived with his repeated hospital admissions for bipolar over many years. I don't think she ever thought it would happen to one of her sons. One of my mom's friends who knew me would later say, "Johnny went off to college and came back a completely different person."

That was not the way it was supposed to be.

Hospital for the Dead

It might as well have been called "The State Hospital for the Dead." I felt I had arrived dead, then left the same way. I met with a psychiatrist. Since drugs were a common cause of admissions, and since I didn't have a history of psychotic breaks, he assumed I took something. I honestly couldn't remember taking anything, but he persisted. The conversation always came back to the doctor wanting to know what drug I had taken. He had the right idea, but I think I would have "gone crazy" anyway even if I had not taken the amyl nitrite or had been slipped the LSD. With all the stressors of my college freshman year, away from home for the first time, my abject lack of skills to deal with them, and my genetic predisposition to bipolar disorder, circumstances acted as triggers.

I would eventually end up in another facility, but my short stay in the "mind factory" proved to be interesting. At admissions, they explained to my mother that it was in my best interests to be admitted voluntarily rather than as an involuntary commitment. It looks better on your record if you're voluntary. You would think it would be an open-and-shut thing. Not so with someone who was now required to sign the commitment papers. For some nebulous reason, only known to myself at the time, I wouldn't approve. It took the admissions lady and my mom about twenty minutes to get me to sign the papers.

I was off to the men's section. I remember wandering the halls. I had a nasty cold, and my nose was running like a fountain. I noticed that many of the other "inmates," otherwise known as patients, would stand facing the wall, walk up close to it for a few seconds, and then turn around with a lit cigarette. Back in the good old days, they let patients smoke in these hospitals. What the guys were doing was lighting their cigarettes on little lighters built into the walls. They were just like old-time car cigarette lighters; at least they didn't give the clientele matches. That was a fine diversion for me, but I was still searching for Kleenex. The snot was getting all over my sleeves and hands. I asked a couple of staff members for some tissues, but nothing was forthcoming. I went into the day room. Still no tissues! I couldn't take it anymore. I snapped, picked up a bookcase full of books, and threw it across the room.

I got tissues after that! They put me in the rubber room so I couldn't hurt anybody or myself. I had never done anything remotely like that in my life. For a minute I became a deranged superhero. Needless to say, I received a medication adjustment and now became more of a pathetic wandering zombie than a superhero, but at least I wasn't throwing bookcases around.

One other noteworthy event happened in "Hellville." I was sleeping when I felt something strange on my thigh. Two of the institution's "finest" male orderlies had come into my room and had started molesting me while I slept. I let out quite a scream, and they disappeared.

I was a guest of the state for about three days while Mom was waiting for a bed to become available at a private hospital. It would be the same private hospital that Dad, who was bipolar, was in at the time. When the discharge person gave me back the envelope of possessions they were holding for me at admission, my high school class ring and the beautiful watch my parents gave me for graduation—the two things that meant the most to me—were missing. I couldn't help but wonder what was going to happen to the people in that place and about the people who could never leave.

We drove about a half hour to a private psychiatric hospital. The place turned out to be a country club compared to the hellhole. There were patients with various problems in different stages of recovery. One girl, a little older, befriended me, and we spent a lot of time in her room, listening to records. She was what I imagine a big sister would be. Her red hair was in a pixie cut, and she was kind of cute. We talked about getting out of the hospital and picking up the pieces back home. For the first time, the intense isolation that comes with mental illness started to decrease. The time I spent with her and our conversations helped ground me. She was my first friend for so long and the first good thing that happened since the "pirates" got me. I wonder what she is doing today. I will always be thankful to her; she helped me find my way back. They say social interaction is good for recovery and staying well. I agree with that.

I met with various doctors and specialists to determine whether my illness might be physical or mental. They checked brain waves and my head for a tumor. Finding nothing in my head—oh, you know what I mean—they concluded that my problem was mental. I could have told them that. The problem was, they had no idea why I was ill. Lacking a better course of action, they thought electric shock treatments would be just the right thing to "jolt" me back to reality. They proceeded with a series of six or eight treatments.

Before the first treatment, I was scared. I didn't know what to expect. I was in my room when the doctor and nurse came in. They were pleasant and matter-of-fact. They asked me if I had any questions or concerns. I asked if they thought this was necessary and if it really would help me. They said they had done the procedure on thousands of patients with excellent results, I wouldn't feel a thing, and it would take about ten minutes. The doctor explained the electric current would be applied to my head for a brief time, from milliseconds to six seconds, and a muscle relaxant would prevent my body from convulsing. I said I had seen a somewhat frightening machine in the hallway that I thought was the shock machine. They said I must have seen the vacuum cleaner, and they brought in the ECT (Electric Convulsive Therapy) machine, which was a small harmless-looking thing. We all had a nervous laugh. The nurse started an IV, and the doctor gave me the anesthesia. I felt a warmth come over my body, and I peacefully went to sleep. When I woke up, I was a little confused about where I was and what time it was, but that passed quickly. There was some trouble remembering events that occurred weeks or months before the procedure, but the trade-off was well worth it to get better.

I still get a twinge when I see a vacuum cleaner, and electric outlets are a little scary. Much later, I would see the macabre irony in the fact that my brain was shocked to rescue it, and someday I would be shocking hearts to save patients. The shock treatments rescued me because, without them, I might have remained in an eternal state of mindless nothingness, better known as insanity.

The treatments progressed and became part of my routine. The mania was starting to subside, and as they adjusted my medications, there was real improvement. I was beginning to make sense and become more aware of myself, my surroundings, and returning to what some would call normal. In about a week, I went home. Without the shock treatments, it might have taken months to get well.

When I got out of the hospital, it was like being dropped back into a place where time continued after I left. I could not tell how much time had passed. I could not fit myself back in time. I didn't know if the people I used to know were the same or gone. I thought a neighbor I knew well was somebody else. It was a confusing time.

I was so depressed I would sleep twelve hours, still not wanting to get out of bed, and when I finally did, I would watch TV for an hour and then take a two-hour nap. Back in bed at night, I would cry uncontrollably for no apparent reason. Driving to doctors' appointments, I would pull over on the highway to cry. I lived in fear a State Trooper would stop and I'd have no explanation, certainly not a comfortable situation to put him in. Time would pass so agonizingly slow that minutes turned into tormented hours of fears and deepening depression. I had an overwhelming feeling that I was living in a sticky capsule of cold molasses and it would never end. Would time ever adjust and become real again? I didn't know if things would ever get back to the way they were before. As the time drag continued endlessly, I thought the only relief might be suicide. The fear of pain and the possibility of missing something should I ever start to feel better again stopped me.

On the flip side, there were weeks or months of untreated mania, which led to psychosis, commonly known as madness. Mania often goes unrecognized because in the beginning it is not full-blown mania but a milder mania known as hypomania. Hypomania can be fun. The person appears more productive, happy, and engaged. A manic person may have inappropriate behavior and speech. Treatment may be needed before it leads to a break in reality as it did for me. I couldn't think straight, comprehend, or communicate effectively. I wasn't hearing voices, but I thought the radio and TV were talking directly to me and telling me what to do. I was paranoid. When I could drive, I thought I was being followed, not only from behind but from the front. I was afraid to leave the house. I couldn't sleep or read. At least my delusions were positive. I always thought that people were assigned to follow me around to protect me.

My shock treatments were many years ago, and there have been improvements over time. I understand they are still effectively used for severe depression, mania, and catatonia, especially when other treatments don't work. Thanks to movies and misperceptions, shock treatments have a stigma like so many other aspects of mental illness. The film *One Flew Over the Cuckoo's Nest* with Jack Nicholson did for shock treatment what *Jaws* did for sharks. I know it helped me. I think of the treatment as a brain reset giving me a chance at life. I'll take that every time. I believe most people would be grateful for some relief from horrible symptoms that can make life unbearable. Shock treatment may be something for you and your doctor to consider if nothing else works.

Although I have had setbacks and relapses, I am fortunate not to have spent any additional time in a mental hospital in almost fifty years. You could say "Been there, done that," but since I came back from that, I live with the constant fear that my mind will leave me and never return. I can't say goodbye. I live every day to its wondrous maximum for as long as I'm here.

Turning Point in Princeton

After my breakdown at college and subsequent two psychiatric hospital stays, nobody quite knew what was wrong with me. I was incorrectly diagnosed twice with schizophrenia by two separate doctors. They saw me at my most psychotic times. I still had a long way to go.

I was sitting around my parents' house, watching TV all day and sleeping way too much. When I was in my room, I spent a lot of time crying. Decades later, my younger brother, who was about sixteen or seventeen at the time, said, "I was right there with you, Bro." He would lie in bed, listening to my bipolar dad and me crying. When my brother sees me now, he still thinks about those nights. He's always been there for me. It's not easy having a sick brother.

From looking at my experience at the mental hospitals and my current mental state, my family doctor also concluded that I was schizophrenic, and that was something he definitely was not equipped to treat. He referred me to a psychiatric research center in the southern part of New Jersey where he had heard a doctor was doing experimental research in conjunction with the Schizophrenia Foundation, using huge doses of various vitamins to treat schizophrenia. Up to that point, there had not been many effective treatments developed for the disorder. I became an outpatient in trials for a mega-vitamin approach as a new treatment for this frightening and devastating disorder. As an outpatient, I would drive down to the research center, meet with a psychiatrist, and be prescribed massive doses of many different vitamins. I was bringing home a shopping bag full of various vitamins and given a regime of how to take them. As the months passed, that approach didn't do anything to improve my symptoms.

Eventually a new young psychiatrist came on board, and after we had met for a while, he determined that I was not schizophrenic but bipolar. It was nice to finally have the correct diagnosis. It had been over three years and two hospitals. He promptly started me on a mood stabilizer, and over a few months, I improved and became more stable. I was even able to volunteer to help in the research lab, assisting the technicians with some simple tests. I gratefully thanked the doctor. It's a shame the vitamin project didn't turn out to be a cure, but it did make me more conscious of how important nutrition is to staying well.

The doctor asked me if I would be willing to check out a new halfway house that was being started in Princeton for young people who had schizophrenia, bipolar, and a host of other serious mental problems. I would be one of the first two patients at the new facility. I was living with Mom and Dad about forty-five minutes north, so it would be an easy commute. Since I was one of the first patients, all expenses at the house would be covered, including treatment and meals. As I look back on it, maybe they gave me a break because I was broke. I had volunteered to be a guinea pig again and hoped it would be more successful than the mega-vitamins.

The halfway house was located along a canal in the countryside outside of Princeton. It was a large remodeled farmhouse with some acreage and a barn. It looked like a beautiful place to be. It reminded me of life as a kid growing up near farms where I rode my bike on country roads and had adventures in farmers' barns around Valley Forge, Pennsylvania. I was greeted at the door by the only other patient. A tall, gangly young girl with short sandy-blond hair. Her name was Sammie, and she had a big welcoming smile and a warm personality. Later I would learn that she had also been diagnosed as schizophrenic. Sammie introduced me to the director, a classy well-dressed professional woman named Barbara. Right from the start, I liked them and couldn't help but like the well-appointed country home, light-years away from the state mental hospital. During the day, the three of us prepared dinner and sat down at a massive solid wood dining room table. Barbara explained that she wasn't a doctor, which was fine by me. So far, about half the doctors who had treated me had come up with the wrong diagnosis. Maybe someone with common sense could get it right. I never did find out what her qualifications were. All I know is that she helped turn my life around. She was a compassionate leader and set a good example.

There we were, the three of us having a good old time. I

drove to the house almost every day. Before it opened, there were people scheduled to live at the house on a full-time basis. I was to be the only outpatient. In about a week, more young people started to arrive, and it was fun meeting everyone. We were birds of a feather, trying to get well.

The young residents consisted of schizophrenics, depressives, bipolars, obsessive-compulsives. A lot of the kids acted spoiled and entitled. As I got to know some of them, it turned out that most came from wealthy families. A few patients were kids or grandkids of the owners or founders of corporations that were household names. We were not supposed to know the last names of the patients because of privacy and security concerns. I got to be friends with a young lady there, and one of her other friends told me who she was. I had never had a friend before who was a billionaire heiress. It looked to me like some well-connected people were sending their sick and somewhat embarrassing kids to the house. I thought these kids seemed a little too well dressed to be the typical twentysomethings I was used to.

As far as treatment goes, I had some great talks with Barbara but nothing I would classify as proper psychiatric counseling. I was still seeing my psychiatrist at the research center. I'm not sure what the other kids were doing for treatment, but the atmosphere of the house and Barbara's empathetic and intuitive guidance seemed to benefit everyone. We did have some problems though. Occasionally someone refused to come out of their room to eat. Incredibly divergent personalities from completely outgoing and manic to almost catatonic often made dinners interesting and sometimes bazaar. Once in a while, somebody would lose control at the table and refuse to eat or start throwing food. Barbara always managed to negotiate a solution so the meal could continue.

About two weeks after the opening of the halfway house, when eight or nine of us were having dinner, Barbara asked if we had any ideas for a name for the new facility. There were a couple of suggestions from other patients. A name popped into my head, and I loudly blurted it out. Earth House! The name represented to me why we were all there, to come back from our distorted realities to earth. Barbara instantly liked it, and everyone agreed. That was it! I left my little mark on the world. The house is still going strong today.

Experiences at the house were the start of significant positive changes in my life. Everybody was assigned chores, including keeping their room tidy, general housekeeping, helping prepare and serve meals, and gardening. Barbara was very strict in a fair way, and it was the first time in my life I had real structure and responsibility. I came from a family of seven, including five challenging children, where there was little structure. I rarely followed my parents' rules.

Barbara was continually thinking up activities for everybody. We had a rowboat on the canal, and we played lots of cards and board games. The property itself had gardens and lush fields. One of my best memories was watching my friend Sammie running through a field of wildflowers. It could have been one of those artsy TV commercials, and for a little while, we forgot how sick we were. I started feeling not so alone, and the stigma of my madness seemed to wane. The place had the air of a resort more than that of a halfway house to recover from severe mental disorders.

As the weeks and months progressed, my symptoms got better and better. The correct diagnosis of bipolar by the young doctor at the psychiatric research center and the right medication was essential. Sometimes it can take months or years for an accurate diagnosis and constant medication adjustments to stay stabilized. Just as crucial was the continual support and encouragement at the halfway house. I was changing. I started making more friends back home and developing new interests.

The halfway house in Princeton was a turning point in my life. I came into the house with almost nothing and left with tools that helped me manage my bipolar. The socialization helped reduce my isolation, and I gained some social skills. Today my wife still says not enough social skills. The structure of daily chores and responsibilities helped ground me then, and structure continues to ground me when my symptoms recur today. Structure also helps keep symptoms at bay. The guidance and empathy from Barbara enabled me to talk openly about my illness for the first time and begin to take responsibility for myself. It gave me the distinct feeling I had possibilities other than madness. It made me well enough to deal better with life and be confident to want to make a difference again. As I left the house in Princeton behind, I knew I had found special people. Special people would help me again in the future. I would need them.

Years later, it would turn out that the first two patients at the house, Sammie and I, would go into the medical field. Sammie became a physician, and I became a paramedic. Maybe we both saw how medicine saved us and we wanted to help others.

The Gift of Music

Things started to change for me when I saw a psychiatrist regularly and was given a mood stabilizer and antipsychotic meds. I was living at home with my parents and was slowly getting better. I started seeing a counselor who helped guide me through a behaviorist approach to coping. We worked closely with my psychiatrist. It was nice to have someone to talk with who was impartial and understanding. As I felt better and stronger, I started leaving the house and socializing with my friends. My old friends accepted me back. I was fortunate. Sometimes friends don't know how to relate to someone recently out of a psychiatric hospital. I'm grateful to them. My counselor said socialization is important because it helps prevent the isolation mental illness can bring.

I was at the beginning of a series of bipolar ups and downs about every year or two. There were many stresses which probably triggered many of the ups and downs. Getting new jobs, being fired, trying to move out of my parents' house, unsuccessful dating. Most young people face these, but they can trigger bipolar episodes. Sometimes there were no triggers, just a chemical imbalance in my brain. It was a life of failures. Yes, the grinding failures happened. I think that's why, when I wasn't ill or failing, I crammed as much living into the spaces of relative normalcy that were given to me. I was very rarely unhappy with this life but rather extraordinarily happy for the time I had. I was not going to be beaten down and pity myself.

I started learning the triggers that can lead to relapse, including inconsistent schedules, poor sleep, poor nutrition, skipping meds, overstimulation, lack of exercise. Life changes such as school, jobs, or personal relationships can also be triggers. It would turn out that those same triggers would last for the rest of my life, and medication would be a daily ritual. Through my decades of bipolar, I would find these triggers and treatments would show up in an uncanny regular way. If I got overconfident or exceedingly depressed and chose not to stick to my long-term treatment plan, I would invariably pay the price of instability. The price was always the feeling of repetitive failure that ended with nothing but backtracking at work or in social situations.

I eventually gathered myself together and made it over to my childhood friend's house. It was great seeing Nate as it brought back memories before my breakdown. We were hanging around in his room. He was playing really well on the guitar. I was amazed to see he had hung a big picture of himself on his own bedroom wall. I never saw anyone put such large pictures of themselves on the wall. He wanted to be a star. That's showbiz!

I had been fast friends with Nate since grammar school. Nate was Jewish, and his parents thought I was also Jewish, which was why I think they liked me. My "cute" little suburban community discriminated against everyone except white Anglo-Saxon Christians, so I guess Nate's parents were glad their son found a friend of the same faith. The only problem was at the time I was Catholic. Nate fancied himself as a budding actor. In high school, he was in the drama club and played the lead in the senior play, *Harvey*. He was really talented. Nate was excellent on the guitar. Turns out, he had an outstanding singing voice. He was even taking voice lessons at the time. I had been fooling around with a set of bongo drums for a while and used to attend all-night jam sessions, playing the conga drum and bongos. The jam sessions were a blast, but no one was very good.

One night we went out to a Mexican restaurant along the highway. The food wasn't that great, but Nate wanted to see something he had heard about. They had a Latin singer going from table to table. He was singing whatever he wanted and he also took requests. Nate and I were fascinated. What a great way to make money, doing something you'd probably do around the house. I'd say, in about two tacos time, Nate and I had hatched a plan right then and there. What a better way to break into show business than playing a glorified taco joint. We spoke to the manager, who said his regular singer was leaving. I'm sure he had been signed by a major label. Maybe not. Anyway, Nate and I got the job. He would only pay us what he paid the one guy. What did we care? This was fantastic!

We had about a week to practice before our first gig. Good thing I was a master percussionist; someone had to back Nate up. My friend knew almost any song you could name, and what he didn't know, he could fake. I played a soft background on the bongos as we went from table to table at the restaurant. We weren't nervous at all. Nate was gregarious and very approachable. Most of the customers liked us, but it didn't matter. We were having the time of our lives and thought we were really getting over with such a sweet gig.

We did have one incident though. There was a group of about six guys sitting around a big table. Generally, we would skip an all-male group as we focused on playing romantic ballads for couples or maybe a light, airy Latin tune. They called us over. They proudly announced that they were Marines on leave. They asked us to play the "Marines' Hymn." Nate and I looked at each other, and I saw the concern on Nate's face for the first time. He had never played it but could wing it. Was it appropriate to play this on guitar and bongos? We didn't have a choice, the Marines insisted. We did our respectful best, but the look on their faces told everything. This was the hymn that represented the Corps. Let's say it didn't translate well on guitar and bongos. We slunk away. If we had tails they would have been between our legs.

We played at a couple of other restaurants for about six months. Our fame was fleeting but fabulously fun. Nate would eventually go on to become a professor at Seaton Hall University, ironically enough a Catholic school. He did kind of end up performing in front of people.

Whether you create music or listen to music, it is a gift available for everyone. If you haven't already opened your gift, do it now. I doubt you'll want to return it. Music always makes me feel better. It can take me back, forward, or be with me now. When I listen to my favorite songs, I feel less isolated. So many times, I can relate to what the artist is saying. It helps me see that others go through the same thoughts and experiences that I do. Sometimes the lyrics are masterpieces of poetry. Many of the works have the power to soothe me when everything around me is in manic confusion or in the vise grip of depression. All my emotions, feelings, and desires can be found in the gift. Through the years, music has had a profound effect on me. Many of the artists that I have listened to seemed like personal friends. The songs that touch me become a part of my loneliness. When something strikes just right, I listen to it over and over again, assimilating every drop of understanding and inspiration. Ever since humans sat around shimmering fires thousands of years ago, we have shared and communicated with each other with the gift of music.

Striking Out

As the months went by, I worked at a car wash and was fired for what the owner said was "a bad attitude." He was right. I couldn't see myself working with a soapy sponge for the rest of my life. This job would only be one in a long series of jobs, which for the most part, were failures.

I started working for a local carpenter who did everything from hanging Sheetrock to roofing. I loved wood-shop in high school and produced some lovely wooden bowls and lamps. I thought working for a carpenter would be like woodshop in high school, and there would be more woodworking. I hoped it would lead to something I could stick with and have pride in. My new boss always wanted me to do ladder and roofing work, knowing I was afraid of heights. He thought I could pull myself up by my bootstraps and get over my fear. His son thought it was funny and laughed at my phobia. It was miserable working with them.

I had managed to accumulate some money, so I thought I would give my parents a break and strike out on my own. A high school friend had an apartment in the city and said there was a studio unit available in his building for not a lot of money. I moved in and set up my one-room household. After about three months, my digs consisted of a mattress on the floor, refrigerator, one window, a bath, kitchenette, and a closet. All this was pretty much in arm's reach. Perfect! Things didn't go like they were supposed to go. I lost my job. Not sure if I quit or was fired, probably fired. Soon after that, I ruined the refrigerator, and most of my food went bad. It was an older fridge that didn't have a defrost mode. Ice would accumulate around the freezer compartment. In a few weeks, it would be two or three inches thick. It couldn't even fit one ice tray. Talented mechanical engineer that I was, I took a screwdriver and a hammer to it. I got some ice off but not before I ruptured the freon line. The coolant for the entire unit rapidly shot out and evaporated. I now had a food closet. I needed a pantry anyway! I had to buy a new used fridge.

I wasn't able to find another job, and my money ran out. I got behind in the rent for a month or two. The landlord applied my initial rental deposit to the back rent. When two full months accumulated, I thought I might be in trouble. I guess I was. One afternoon when I came back to my apartment, my key didn't work. The landlord had changed the lock. I thought this was poor form on his part. He didn't warn me or even leave a note. All my stuff was in there. How was I supposed to move out? Granted, my stuff had a total value of about $200, but it was my stuff! Besides, he got a brand "new" used fridge out of the deal. It seemed to me the landlord was a bit petty and vindictive by making my life harder than it already was. He didn't even give me an eviction notice so I could have moved my stuff out. I felt pathetic that I could not keep a cheap apartment consisting of a mattress and a refrigerator without getting evicted. I had struck out.

I moved back home, and it wouldn't be long until the bipolar psych genie made an appearance. You won't believe how little time it took me to start ignoring what I learned at the halfway house. Not only that but to quickly develop into a real dumbass that didn't have a lick of common sense. I was bored and boring. I ate a lot of junk food like Hostess Snowball cupcakes, Coke, and Milano cookies. I wasn't exercising unless you count the one chore to take out the trash and occasionally babysit my youngest brother. At no point did I take on any responsibility for myself. I didn't even keep to a strict medication schedule. I was lucky I had a place to go. If it wasn't for my parents, I am absolutely sure I would have ended up living in a box on the street in San Francisco, a psych ward, jail, a combination of all three, or dead.

2

HAVING TOO MUCH FUN

I JUST WANTED EVERYTHING HANDED TO ME AND TO have fun. That fun, which may be entertaining, sometimes is a malignant progression from hypomania to full-blown mania or psychosis. It may start out fun and barely noticeable but can progress to inappropriate risky behavior and eventually become out of control and reckless, destructive behavior. After my "career" in music, I was beginning to enter a manic phase of my bipolar disorder. It started out fun but became more and more risky and irresponsible with each exploit.

Under Arrest

I was on a date with a college girl a little younger than me, who was home for the summer. She lived in Short Hills, one of the poshest areas of the state. She lived in a mansion with an expansive manicured yard and a four-car garage. For our first date, we were going to the movies, an innocent-enough activity. I told her dad I would have her home by eleven. She was tall and rather busty. That was fine by me. We went to the movie and had a little time before her curfew. Being an ex-scout, I was prepared. I had brought two bottles of cheap German wine. After the movie, we drove around until we found a large field of very tall grass. We promptly proceeded to the middle of the field and set a blanket down. Well, after one bottle, we were making out pretty well, but after the second, the fun really started. I think we started getting louder. We lost track of time. You know how time flies.

I remember we were drunk, stumbling down the dirt road, looking for my car. It was a pitch-black night with no streetlights or moon. We literally walked into my car, tripping over it, at which time the night was suddenly lit up by the flashing light rack on the patrol car parked in front of my car. Two officers got out and shined their flashlights right in our eyes. Blinded, disoriented, and intoxicated, I was informed that I was under arrest for trespassing. Apparently, we were making enough noise to bother the people in a house near the field. For a brief moment, I felt like quite the stud. That moment passed remarkably fast as the cops asked me to empty my pockets. I was a little startled when one of them called me by name. I hadn't given him my license yet. Turns out, they had already been through my car and had my information. I don't know how long they were waiting for us to come out of the field, but it must have been a while. I didn't have much in my pockets, but I was carrying two empty bottles of wine. Actually, I was a little proud that we didn't leave the bottles behind. I might have been a trespasser, but at least I wasn't a litterbug. I guess it was my winning smile or the fact that we hadn't robbed a bank or anything that they let us go. They probably remembered they were young and stupid once, which likely played a factor in our timely release.

When I finally got my date back home, it was almost three a.m., a little later than the eleven p.m. I had discussed with her dad. The worried parents waited up, and you could say it was an ugly scene as we tried sneaking up the steps through the garage door entrance. He grabbed his daughter and shoved me down the steps and hit the garage door button before I was even close to getting out. I imagined myself captive in the garage and subjected to horrible angry father tortures. It didn't have an electric eye shut off, so I was almost caught under the rapidly closing door.

My evening wasn't quite over yet. A really dense fog had set in from my date's house all the way home. The police must have radioed ahead as a cop at each town I drove through stopped me with his light rack flashing. The fog was so dense I could hardly see their lights. Each of them asked me for my license and registration. They told me to keep it slow and be careful. Now that I think about it, they were my guardian angels that night. I was lost and terribly drunk. There was no GPS at the time. This little game of theirs continued as they pulled me over in each of the three towns I had to go through to get home to my parents' house. I often wonder why they didn't arrest me for drunk driving. I guess they figured they were young and stupid once too, or was it my winning smile?

The Girl and the Microbus

I started dating a girl named Betty, who was the sister of a friend of my ex-girlfriend. We mostly hung out at her sister's, who worked for VISTA, Volunteers in Service to America. That was a kind of domestic Peace Corps. When we weren't at her house, we generally spent most of our time in the woods, hiking and doing other fun things that couples do.

A bunch of mutual friends decided they were going to take a VW Microbus from our town in New Jersey to Boulder, Colorado. They said we could come along if we wanted. I was probably a little manic at the time, but that was an offer too good to pass up. I had always wanted to see the Rockies.

Neither one of us had jobs, so there was no reason not to go. Wow! I went from living at home with my parents to moving to Boulder with a girl I had only known for a couple of weeks. Manic you say? I guess so.

My parents weren't thrilled about that, especially with my ongoing psychiatric challenges, but they knew enough to know that I pretty much always did what I wanted. I compromised a little and agreed to buy a one-way airline ticket home from Denver, so if I ran out of money or got into trouble, I could always make it back. As it turned out, I was glad my dad thought of that.

We set out in the bus and had a grand time talking and laughing. Betty and I asked if we could help with the driving, but the two guys in the front wanted to handle it. For most of the two-day trip, Betty and I ended up on a thin mattress in the back wrapped up in a large sleeping bag. I can't think of a better existence. I never realized how flat Kansas was and how friendly the people were at the Dairy Queen along the highway, where I had the best milkshake of my life. It was smoother, richer, and colder than any other milkshake I ever had. We saw a fantastic double rainbow on the faraway Kansas horizon with colors that Disney couldn't have made more vivid. When I was manic, everything seemed to taste better and look better.

We arrived in Boulder in the early evening. A couple of others who had already made the trip and established a residence in a big old Victorian house met us at the curb. It was a warm hearty greeting that led to a great party. The house was on Canyon Boulevard, one of the main streets in town leading into the Rocky Mountains. I couldn't believe it. Here I was at a place I dreamed of. At the base of the majestic Flatirons rock formations in a magical mountain town. I was at the end of that rainbow!

Everybody at the house got along and helped each other out when they could. Jobs were pretty scarce because there was a lot of competition with the kids at the University of Colorado, which was within walking distance. There was one car and the Microbus for transportation, but we hardly ever found work, so we didn't need additional transportation. Some in the group had savings or were getting money from home. We qualified for food stamps, and when they were finally issued, we ate really well for a while. Every so often, the government food stamp people would come to the house to inspect our food setup. They required each of us to keep our own food separate from everyone else's food. So in each cabinet, we had to keep our individual food from touching someone else's items. This seemed like a Cracker Jack system the government had come up with to employ food separation inspectors.

The only semblance of conflict in Boulder turned out to be between Betty and me. We had our own room and were happy as clams until one night Betty dragged in a stray cat to bed. I thought this was kinda cute until she said it was going to sleep in our bed all night. I couldn't handle a stinky old cat all night. We argued about the cat, and after Betty went to sleep, I took the cat and put it on the roof of the house. There was a low point of the roof, and I thought the cat could get down from there. That was not my finest hour. The next day she found the unharmed cat right outside our door. Betty and the cat moved out to live with her brother across town.

I was not deterred. I had wondrous things to see and do in Boulder, consisting of walking and hitchhiking all over the city. I visited the university and noticed how healthy and vibrant the students looked. I went into a couple of classroom buildings and sat in on a class. I think it was psychology. How ironic. I went to the bookstore and the student union. What a fabulous place to go to school in the shadow of snowcapped mountains. I stopped at a health food shop and had a glass of cold carrot juice. I never had anything so good except for that milkshake in Kansas.

As they say, "There was a fly in the ointment." It couldn't

last forever. In about a month, I had run out of money. I had to say goodbye to my friends on Canyon Boulevard and hitch to Denver for a flight back to New Jersey. I must have been a little manic on my trip to Boulder. I had hoped to move there but instead had my third failure to launch after college and my first apartment.

Years later, with my beautiful wife, I would return to the Rockies that I loved and live in one of the snowiest, coldest mountain towns in the country, spending many Christmases visiting Boulder.

By the way, our dog sleeps with us today.

Let's Party

When I was living with my parents again, I started dating Nancy from another town and took her to a party in my neighborhood. I had met her at Earth House several years ago, and we were both struggling to find our way. My mania was progressing, and I was speaking faster and more than ready for some fun that might not have been well thought out. We had a lot in common; she was bipolar also and had a taste for tequila. It was standard procedure when somebody's parents were out of town to throw a big party. You'd invite friends, and they would invite their friends, and when word got out, lots of strange and wonderful people would show up. When we got there, it was going full tilt, and we started mingling. I was doing shots of "crazy juice" with beer to wash it down. As I walked into the kitchen, I ran into an old girlfriend from high school. We were both normally shy and quiet, but we were both drinking and I was manic. It wasn't long till I found her on my lap. We were reminiscing and flirting. That didn't go over well with Nancy, and when I finally looked around for her, I didn't see her.

Soon it was time to get Nancy home. I checked all over the house, the front and backyard. No Nancy. I asked everybody. I was afraid if she had taken a walk and might have gotten lost because she was from out of town. I had lost my date! Would I have to call the police? As I was walking past my car looking for her, I noticed the windows were fogged up. When I looked in the window, low and behold, there was Nancy with one of my best friends, going at it. I tapped on the window, but they didn't miss a beat. I very rarely get angry, but when she got back to the party, I was furious. I told her she could find another ride home. My friend that she had hooked up with didn't have a car, and she didn't know anybody at the party. There, that would fix her! It was getting late. Eventually I realized I had also been a dope at the party, ignoring her and drinking too much. My guy friend's behavior wasn't stellar either. It was time to take her home.

Nancy and I were both bipolar, who happened to be in hypomanic states at the time. Not in full-blown psychosis of mania but in the speeded-up hypomanic state where too much fun and poor decisions happen. On top of that, we had been drinking. All my meds had warnings not to drink while using them. No problem. Unlike my normally shy self, I was an immortal twentysomething. Throw in tequila and horny, and you can see trouble brewing. My friend happily took advantage of the situation. The takeaway is that during a manic phase, many with bipolar do things they generally wouldn't do. Feeling too good, invincible, and powerful can lead to risky behaviors and promiscuousness. Not counting the drunk driving or being a dumbass, luckily I didn't break any laws at the party except for social norms.

The Prostitute

I've never been able to take back the bad. If you find out how, let me know. The hypomania, which could have led to full-blown mania and psychosis, continued on a rapidly winding course because I didn't know enough to recognize what was happening and changing me. It is a time when so much speeds up; thoughts, speech, and sex drive can quicken. It had progressed to the point where I didn't really care what I did, impulse took over, and everything appeared to be so much fun. Hypomania was progressing and had a solid hold on me now. I found it hard to keep it in my pants.

I met a young prostitute named Kit, who had long red hair and couldn't have weighed more than ninety pounds. She showed me a picture of herself before she started drugs. Now with a ten-bag-a-day heroin habit and smoking forty hits of crack a day, I never would have guessed it was her. Even being so thin and addicted to heroin, Kit was remarkably beautiful, but she was the kind of girl whose license plate number you leave with a friend in case you turn up missing.

The most fun we ever had was when I took her down to the county courthouse to pay a fine. I assumed I knew what for. Anyway, while we were passing one of the courtrooms, she stopped and said she knew someone at one of the trials. She opened the big oak doors and stood at the entrance. The proceedings stopped momentarily as all eyes turned to the striking woman at the door. She waved to the county prosecutor who was standing near the witness box, and he instantly turned white and did an about-face. She quickly closed the door, and we disappeared down the crowded hall. She had such a sly look of joy on her face. Turns out, the prosecutor was one of her clients. Being with this girl was fun and exciting.

She had some bad points, to say the least. I was up in her room in a boarding house, looking through her coloring books and poems, when she said she had to go see her aunt, who was renting one of the other rooms in the boarding house. I always kept my wallet in the car. I'm not crazy; she was a nice person but a crack whore on heroin. When I got home, I checked my wallet. I always keep $120 in it, but it was empty. While I was occupied in her room, she had gone down to my car and took the money. Next time I saw her, I confronted her with my suspicion, but she denied it, saying, "On the life of my son, I didn't take it." I didn't know if she even had a son. About a week later, her cousin told me Kit took the money and bragged about it. He also warned me to stay away from her because she would never change and I seemed like a nice guy. Making yet another manic poor decision, I forgave her. She was such a believable con artist. Like many heroin addicts, she would lie, cheat, and steal to get a fix.

The last I heard from her was when she called from the car she was now living in and said I had to give her $500, or she would tell my employer about my debauchery. I told her to go ahead; my boss knew I was a jerk. I wonder if her lawyer-client at the courthouse paid up.

Why did I put up with those behaviors? I don't know. Maybe it was because I liked having a perverted sexual adventure, or perhaps I thought I could have ended up in the same desperate situation if I was in her place. Or maybe being hypomanic I was just not making good decisions. Many times addicts have an underlying psychiatric problem on top of addiction. My call girl told me she had been in jail many times and was in thirteen rehab programs. She was kicked out of most of them for dealing drugs to the other patients. The rescuer in me felt a need to help her, but I hadn't known where to begin.

I have bipolar friends with similar stories of uncharacteristic things they did during a manic phase. Impulses can run wild. My bipolar dad bought flashy cars and even purchased another house without my mom's knowledge when he was manic. Those endeavors can be destructive and create turmoil in a bipolar's already confusing life. Remember, don't try this at home.

The takeaway from my manic escapade is that a lot of mentally ill folks self-medicate or try to escape by taking drugs or alcohol. Seeing what happened to this untreated person woke me up.

You could question the morality and legality of what I did. I wasn't in Nevada, Amsterdam, or Australia, where it's legal. My flimsy excuse is my hypomania. I didn't think my actions through or even cared much about consequences. If you carry this behavior forward to extremes, it becomes apparent that mania can be a real problem.

When I start getting manic, I make little mistakes like forgetting my keys or an appointment. Small mistakes become bigger until eventually I find myself in a peck of trouble. I have to consciously break the cycle by taking deep breaths, talking slower, and moving away from stimulating things and people... such as skinny hookers. It's hard work but needs to be done. The manic fun can lead to legal headaches, financial and emotional loss, not to mention an abrupt shift into psychosis and a mental hospital. I was lucky; I had a scheduled check-in appointment with my psychiatrist. I was too close to the problem, but he instantly explained to me what was going on and that it's very common for bipolar patients to enter a manic phase without realizing it. It's fun but insidious. You could say mania can bait you with artificially good things and feelings until you fall into its deep, dark pit of depression with the hooked spikes of loneliness at the bottom that grab you.

Hypomania started out tasting sweet as honey and ended up bitter vinegar. The scary part of hypomania is that for many, if not treated somewhere along the line, it develops into psychosis with hospitalization. The fun stops at crazy. This is not the way it is supposed to be.

It Didn't Blow Up

After the doctor recognized I was manic, he adjusted my medication and was able to stabilize me without another hospital stay. I started going to a coffeehouse at a nearby college and met a small group looking for a large apartment to share. Gary, one of our more enterprising coffeehouse friends, heard that the ex-McGovern headquarters was going to be rented as apartments. McGovern no longer needed it as he had just lost his run for presidency against Nixon by a landslide.

Gary made a deal with the landlord that if we cleaned the place up and did some minor repairs, we could have the four-bedroom place for the first month free. What a sweet deal. When we got the key and tried to get inside, the door was blocked. Old files and papers were piled almost to the ceiling. Phones and some other office equipment were among the clutter. McGovern's campaign workers might not have gotten him elected, but they sure had known how to generate paper.

The four of us got to work. It felt good that we were making our home out of such a mess. A lot of the old windows in the place were broken or painted shut. Gary turned out to be very handy and went to work on each one. He was becoming the leader of our little band of homesteaders. The four of us, three guys and a girl, settled into our new digs, and some of us found jobs. We didn't pay much attention to what our roommates were doing day to day, but we all got along fine and had some meals together.

I was working as a nude model for art classes down at the college. I had answered a classified ad. They didn't seem to mind that I was not handsome or muscular. I think I was the only one who responded to the ad. It certainly wasn't hard work, just a matter of standing or sitting very still for long periods while the students did their best to paint me. It was even a bit of an ego boost until during breaks I would put on a robe and check out their work. I imagined seeing one of those paintings at a garage sale, but I bet my wife wouldn't appreciate it.

Everything was going smoothly. We were making the rent and getting by. Many nights my friend Bobby and I went to the coffeehouse at the college to listen to people read their poems and folk singers play acoustic guitars, but mostly to meet girls. One night there were a couple of really cute girls sitting at a table. It wasn't a big thing to share a table, so we invited ourselves to sit down. Turns out they were sisters, both rather fetching. I started talking to the one I thought was the cutest. It was kind of an arbitrary selection method, but you had to start somewhere. It wasn't long until I came to the realization that I had made the wrong choice. There was no chemistry. Later I would find out how lucky I was that we didn't hit it off.

Bobby wasn't having much luck with the other sister, so we knowingly looked at each other and we switched places and girls. Never say die. Sara, my new companion, had a pretty face, long blond hair, and a great body. As we talked that evening, her appearance started matching up with her intelligence and personality. She was attending college to become a teacher. There was one thing about her that struck me as unusual. She spoke in a monotone, and I couldn't decide if it was strange or sexy. We started dating. I was really getting into the idea of being faithful and became exclusive. Little did I know that this wonderfully strange woman would soon save my life. Sara and I would meet at the coffeehouse a lot and then go over to the apartment. Bobby saw the other sister a couple of times and told me she turned out to be a vindictive, judgmental bitch. I came out ahead on this one.

One day something came up. A couple of us wanted to go to a lecture by the Dali Lama, and a couple of us wanted to go to a party. We broke up into the lecture people and the party people. I went to the lecture and Sara went to the party. The lecture finished, and we heard the party was still going strong. We drove over to the party, and I looked for Sara. I checked the whole downstairs and thought maybe she had left. I asked someone if anyone had seen her and was told she was upstairs with the party's host in his bedroom. Well, this was a fine kettle of fish. I went upstairs and knocked on the door, asking if Sara was there. I heard the sound of a lot of movement and rustling in the room. Before long, she emerged. Her hair was a mess, and her dress was literally on crooked.

We were silent on the ride back to the apartment. We sat on the end of my bed to talk. Without saying a thing, Sara started looking at me with a gigantic shit-eating grin. To both our surprise and amazement, I slapped her across the face, really hard, knocking her to the floor. She started laughing, and for some reason I found myself getting intensely aroused. We made love, never spoke of the incident again, and went on to have a great monogamous relationship. Of course, there would be no more slapping. If you knew me, you would know how much that was out of character. I never slapped anyone again.

Back at the apartment, Gary turned out to be a marijuana dealer. He had a lot of connections and used to bury most of his stash in the backyard. Many of my friends were doing everything from hashish, cocaine, uppers, downers, and LSD. My nickname was Saint John because I was usually the only one not indulging. I had tried to smoke a couple of times, but it did nothing for me. I also didn't think drugs would mix well with my meds, and I didn't want another episode that landed me in the mental hospital.

Gary had hitched over to West Virginia to visit friends. He was gone a week. When he got back, he looked terrible. His hair was matted, he was dirty, and he had lost weight. He said he had partied hard in West Virginia and had a hard time hitching rides back home; understandable, being he didn't look like the ideal travel companion. He said he had been on speed for days and had hardly slept and had no money. His use of speed reminded me of that fateful time I used speed in the form of amyl nitrate, contributing to my first psychotic episode. The day after he was back, one of my roommates announced that her wallet had been stolen. It was determined Gary had stolen the money, and to make everything worse, he was still on speed. He admitted to it and said he had spent the money. Our happy life in the apartment was coming to an end.

The next day I was awakened by a scream the likes I have never heard before. It was Sara. She had let herself in, and when she entered the living room, she discovered Gary, lying on the floor with his head wrapped up tightly in plastic, the natural gas line leading into the bag with the valve wide open. I pulled and ripped the plastic from around his head and face, but it was way too late. Rigor mortis had already set in. The smell of gas was very strong. It generally takes hours for rigor mortis to take effect, so the gas had been going on full for a long time. I told Sara to get out. There was no one else in the apartment.

I ran back to my room and put on a pair of pants. I was considered almost legally blind without my contact lenses, but there was no time to put them in. I ran down the stairs to the street where I found a hysterical Sara. I ran down the sidewalk to get help. Not being able to see much without my contacts, it must have been a lucky fate to run full speed into a policeman walking a beat. I had never seen a cop walking on that street before or since that day. He ran up the stairs and saw and smelled the urgency of the situation and started opening all those windows that were once stuck shut until Gary had fixed them. He told me to get the hell out of there as he bravely opened every window before he left the building. There is no doubt that if there had been a spark or another ignition source, that building would have blown up.

The ambulance came to pick up Gary. I didn't know it at the time, but I would eventually be working for the same ambulance squad.

Later, we learned that Gary was an AWOL soldier living underground. He couldn't work because if he gave his social security number to an employer, it would be flagged and he would be apprehended. The pressure of being a fugitive, taking amphetamines for days, not sleeping, and being caught stealing from a friend was too much for him. If it wasn't for Sara, I would been asphyxiated by the gas or gone up with the building when it blew. She saved my life.

It would be decades before I would have a chance to repay her. After thirty years, I got a call from Sara. She had tracked me down and wanted to talk. It was great to hear from her. How often do you hear from long-lost friends who saved your life? As I listened, it became apparent that she wanted to apologize for abruptly dumping me. She didn't say it, but I think she was making amends as part of the twelve-step program for Alcoholics Anonymous. She was divorced and had two sons, and I had also married. We periodically spoke on the phone through the years. She became an RN and the head nurse in a psychiatric hospital. You'll never guess where she worked; my dear friend now worked in the same state mental health system that included the hellhole of a hospital I found myself in with my first psychotic break. The original state mental hospital where I was first admitted was closed down and bulldozed, and I know the new hospital was much better because she worked there.

One day I'll never forget, she called to tell me she had been diagnosed with rectal cancer. Cancer is no fun, and that particular type can be aggressive and excruciating. The doctors at the cancer center gave her a little over a year and a half. We talked and talked. I knew I would miss her terribly.

She was living in a small apartment in North Jersey, and I was in Connecticut near the Massachusetts border. She had mentioned that she always wanted to see Mystic Seaport. I checked with my wife, and it was okay with her if Sara and I met at Mystic. It was a crisp sun-drenched spring day. We toured some of the famous tall ships, had a great lunch, hit a museum, and took a boat ride. We never spoke of her illness but only of what a beautiful time we were having.

It started getting dark, and we needed to get home. Home to

my wife, Sara home to her cat. We walked arm in arm to the cars. We didn't want to let go. We knew. I could tell she wanted me to kiss her. I was leaning back on her car, we started kissing, and then I spun her around and almost pinned her against the car. We kissed a long goodbye.

3

EMT / PARAMEDIC

Instant Sleep to EMT

AFTER I ESCAPED THE APARTMENT THAT DIDN'T explode, I ended up back home with my parents. I went through a cycle of breakdowns, getting a job, getting fired, collecting unemployment, knocking around, getting a job, getting fired. You get the idea.

I had to show up at the unemployment office every two weeks with a list of at least three prospective employers I had visited personally to apply for a job. Most people never went to three employers but just listed a few on the paperwork they handed in. I'm not saying it's right, just human nature. Anyway, one day I thought I would be honest with the unemployment examiner. I told him I hadn't been to any prospective employers in the past two weeks. He disappeared into a back room, and when he came out, he had a piece of paper burning a hole in his hand. He handed it to me, and in big, bold letters, it said "Claim Denied: Does Not Show a Genuine Attachment to the Labor Market." I don't think there had ever been said a more accurate truth about me. I was not genuinely attached to the labor market in general. I was, however, genuinely attached to labor I liked to do. Turns out, I liked saving lives, but there were not a lot of jobs for a college dropout available in that field.

I had seen the volunteer rescue squad occasionally responding to calls around our town of about 60,000 people. Since I wasn't attached to the labor market, I thought volunteering might be a way to occupy my time. I might even get that feeling back of making a difference in someone's life, like when I was a lifeguard.

I went down to the volunteer ambulance headquarters and spoke to the person at the desk. I filled out an application and gave it back to her. There happened to be a meeting of the squad members in the other room. She took my application to the meeting. As they were always looking for new members, I assumed this would be a shoe-in. After about a half hour the meeting ended, and I thought the organization's president would want to interview me. I waited for another half hour, the desk lady left, and I waited for another half hour. Nobody even acknowledged the fact that I was there. Feeling rejected and desolate, I left.

The only thing I can think of why nobody seemed to want me there was that maybe they knew of my recent mental problems. It was a small enough town that someone at the meeting might have recognized me. Maybe I was acting strangely. I was on a lot of powerful meds. That rejection was hard to take. There was, and still is, a lot of fear and discrimination out there.

It's nice to have plan B, and I did. I would go and get my Emergency Medical Technician certification. If they could see me get advanced training, which was more than most of the members of the squad had, then maybe they would let me join. On the other hand, I thought of the Groucho Marks quote. "I don't want to belong to any club that will accept me as a member."

I got a lot out of being a lifeguard and saving those kids, so I thought becoming an EMT made sense. I signed up at the local community college and started class and liked it right from the start. The course included lectures and practical training. There were about twenty-five students and several instructors. Some of the instructors were EMTs with years of experience, and some were emergency room nurses. The entire course was supervised by a doctor who specialized in emergency medicine. We were issued an orange textbook, which would be our bible. We were expected to understand everything in it and be able to perform all the tasks that were employed to save a life, using the equipment available to us. I sat in the front row, hanging on every word.

This was not like sleeping my way through high school and being known as instant sleep. This EMT stuff was just right for me. It was a challenge and kept getting more and more interesting. I found myself memorizing the text so I would have the material down cold to compensate for the hard times ahead with my illness. Later on while working ambulance calls, there was so much confusion with people bleeding and screaming that I would have to make the right decisions among the chaos and make them fast, or people would die. Having the knowledge at my fingertips made all the difference. When bipolar symptoms came back, I had a reserve of knowledge and experience to fall back on.

During a break one night, I got to talking to a group of students who always came to class together. They said they all worked for Emergency Medical Services in the city. They were there to improve their advanced first aid training to the EMT level. They were members of the ambulance squad that took Gary away. They asked me why I was taking the training, and I said it was an effort to get onto my local volunteer squad. Someone said I should come down and apply for a job with the city ambulance and get paid for something I would do for free.

This chance conversation would be another turning point in my life. At the end of the course, we were required to pass practical skills tests and a three-hour written exam given by the state, and I was awarded my state EMT certificate. I was in my early twenties and had never been awarded anything before. I wasn't done yet.

I learned by those successes and failures that I'm glad I put myself out there. I tried different things. I was kind of like a pinball, bouncing off one thing to another. Sometimes the game can be fun, and you win. Sometimes it's a luckless struggle of failures. The thing is, you have to play the game to have a chance. I've made mistakes, needing apologies to people I have hurt along the way, but if I had never gotten off my butt and played the game, there would be regrets.

Graveyard Shift

I went to work as an ambulance EMT at the Department of Health, City of Elizabeth, New Jersey. Elizabeth is a nitty-gritty, medium-sized city just across the river from New York City. EMTs wore brown pants with a thin orange stripe down the sides and white shirts with a city patch on one sleeve and an American flag on the other. I hadn't worn a uniform since Boy Scouts, and this one felt okay.

I worked the graveyard shift, the busiest shift, eleven in the evening to seven in the morning. This station was one of three in the city. It was in the run-down and dangerous part of town. If you lived there, you would just call it home. Why did I take this job? I wanted to work as an EMT in a rough neighborhood because I was suffering from survivor's guilt. Many of my friends and acquaintances were drafted or enlisted to fight in Vietnam. Too many were coming back in flag-draped coffins.

My psychiatrist had written a letter to the draft board, explaining my condition, and I was issued a psychiatric deferment. I was also almost legally blind without glasses. I wouldn't have been the best shot in the world. A lot of friends were joining the domestic Peace Corps, VISTA, or the international Peace Corps. I had wanted to do public service as far back as when my dad took my brother and me to the John F. Kennedy inauguration. Dad supported every president, no matter which party.

Fresh snow had fallen on the capital, and the whole scene was classic white Washington buildings and monuments highlighted by the beautiful white freshly fallen snow. It was surprisingly hushed and quiet. Hard to imagine the history and fanfare that was about to take place. It was January and so cold my dad wrapped our feet in newspaper to keep them warm. We got to the capital early and stood on the Senate side of the gallery in the front row. We listened to Robert Frost reading his famous poem "The Gift Outright." The glare from the sun was so bright he couldn't see his notes. No problem, he's Robert Frost, one of America's greatest poets. He continued from memory, and it was beautiful.

Other speakers presented, and somewhere along the line of speakers the podium started smoking. The secret service handled it, and then it was Kennedy's turn. I was freezing cold, our feet wrapped in newspapers, but he didn't even wear a hat. I remember his immortal words: "Ask not what your country can do for you; ask what you can do for your country."

Call me crazy, but later when I couldn't go fight for my country in Vietnam, I remembered those words, and at least I could help out at home. Instead of going to war, I could put in my service on the home front. Instead of trying to kill people, I'd try to give people's lives back to them.

The other EMTs were mostly young men and a few women. Everybody was in their twenties or thirties with one guy about forty. I recognized one. By golly, it was an old girlfriend. Sue! You might think that would be a good thing. To have someone you know to be your friend and show you the ropes. No such luck. I had stopped seeing this girl a couple of years ago, and the vindictive little darling tried to have me fired anyway she could. After all that studying and training for this new job, I wasn't going to let Sue have her retribution.

Part of my job was to complete run sheets for each call. The run sheets included run times and everything you did for the patient, including bandaging, splinting, administering oxygen, CPR. My priority was the patient, not the paperwork. Sue was very friendly with the supervisor, and when I came back from a call, she would try to find errors and generally pick them apart. She proceeded to bad-mouth me around the squad. She happened to be sleeping with the supervisor, and they had made an alliance. That was problematic. Here I was at what I had hoped would be my career dream job, and I had these two clucks trying to get rid of me. My only defense was an offense. I became the best at what I did. The overwhelming feeling among my peers was that I was a superior technician. The conflict with Sue helped me to become a better EMT. This also benefited me in the future when anxiety or bipolar feelings came on. I had reserves to fall back on. I was fortunate that I didn't suffer any significant bipolar symptoms when Miss Sue and friend were trying to have me canned. Had that happened, I doubt I could have hung on. I also knew I had to build a good reputation among my coworkers. It was just a matter of time until bipolar symptoms would return. I might need their support. I knew procedures cold, which would help me through chaotic situations without thinking twice.

As the years went by and the calls rolled in, my strategy worked. Sue transferred to another station. I did have some minor symptoms. As I felt the mania coming on, I contacted my psychiatrist, and he adjusted my meds. After I was in the civil service for a number of years, I had a lot of vacation and sick time. I took time off I needed and came back ready to go again. I was getting better and better at recognizing and heading off bipolar episodes. I was in remission. I had become the senior EMT at my station, so at times I would be the station chief. I had three or four ambulances and about fifteen techs. I would handle the 911 calls that were sent directly to my desk from police headquarters. I would talk to the caller, determine the problem, how many ambulances would be needed, then assign and dispatch the crews.

I think back to the little suburban town I came from, the sad and dejected day at the rescue squad when I was left sitting alone wondering what was wrong with me. In my career as an EMT chief/paramedic and a volunteer for the Red Cross as a disaster action team member, I responded to roughly 10,000 calls and disasters. It's a "high" making a direct difference in the lives of so many. Not to mention what fun it was to drive around with lights and sirens. I sincerely believed I was exceptional at what I did and hoped I would have the sense to get out if there came a time that the job started to consume me.

Never Give Up

After working as an EMT for several years, I still had a thirst for adventure, danger, and the satisfaction of helping people. I wanted to go as far in my career as I could. My bipolar periods were still occurring, but I was getting much better at handling them. A good psychiatrist and the right meds were working, so my ups and downs were not as frequent or severe.

I went to the State Rehabilitation Commission, and based on my current success, they offered me a full scholarship to a Registered Nurse (RN) or Paramedic program. Sweet! I did very well on the nursing pre-boards for nursing school and interviewed well for paramedic school. I chose paramedicine because, as an emergency room RN, I would work in the hospital ER with the doctors. I thought it best to avoid someone looking over my shoulder. As a paramedic on an ambulance, I only answered to my patients, not someone's ego.

I didn't accept the scholarship because I figured I was working and someone else could use the money more. I borrowed some money from my dad to finish the program; all that to pursue one of the lowest paying professions in health care. I knew other volunteer paramedics, and I would have done it for free. I started paramedic training, full time during the day, and kept working full-time nights. My original EMT training was a three-month course of eighty hours. Paramedicine training would take two years and two thousand hours.

I still had some bipolar symptoms, and I knew there would likely be trouble during my training. There was no point worrying. I felt obligated to give my patients the best care, and I was beginning to question if I was getting in too deep. I was more than halfway through academic training and starting practical hospital rotations and spent time in almost every department in the hospital, mostly learning by observing. It was a burning hatred that came upon me when the symptoms of bipolar depression started coming back. Was this the end of my dream to be the best in my field? Would I have to give up?

I must have started acting differently because it wasn't long until the emergency room nurse in charge of my training wanted to talk to me. She took me into an operating room that hadn't been used for a while. We stood there. She asked me what was wrong. I told her about my ambulance night work and taking my mother for cancer treatments. I also told her the one thing I never dared tell anyone else, that I was bipolar. She was a true professional, and in the academic courses and dealings I had with her, I had grown to respect her. I was sure she would have to eliminate me from the program. The paramedic concept was new to the state, and my class would be scrutinized closely to see if it would be accepted and implemented statewide. A bipolar person might jeopardize the credibility of the entire program.

We talked for a while, and I will never forget the compassion on her face as she said she would like me to remain in the program. She was absolutely putting her career and possibly the future of the program on the line. That was one of those moments that changed my life. As we left the abandoned operating room, a site unseen orderly climbed down from a high out-of-the-way shelf where he had been furtively napping. He had an embarrassed look on his face as he left. I was afraid he'd overheard our conversation, but he never said anything.

I went to my doctor, and with a medication adjustment, my bipolar episode resolved. My mother's cancer treatments successfully completed. I went on with training, and in about nine or ten more months, it was time for our final written boards and practical tests. We studied nonstop. A few of us formed a study group, meeting regularly. There are plenty of bones and muscles in the human body, and it really helped to quiz each other.

The final written test was five hours long, and the final practice exam consisted of five stations. At each station, there were examiners comprised of a combination of one or two emergency room doctors and two emergency room nurses. The first four stations went pretty well for me, where we treated wounds, diagnosed and treated fractures, handled heart attacks and strokes.

The fifth station was the electrocardiogram, EKG or ECG, heart monitor station. The examiners had me read and interpret multiple paper EKG strips with different heart arrhythmias or abnormalities. I was correct on all until the last strip, which was the final test of the day, in the whole exam. I looked at it and studied the wave patterns. I didn't remember seeing that one anywhere in my training. There was always something! They said, take your time, and I did. I started to visibly sweat. It must have been five minutes with those people watching me. It felt like forever. Through the process of elimination, I could only come up with one answer. Bundle branch block. It was the right answer!

As each of my classmates finished the practical, we all gathered outside to compare notes. It turned out I was the only one to get the bundle branch block EKG strip correct and the only one with a perfect score on the practical.

I had earned my AAS degree from the NJ College of Medicine and Dentistry. I am proud and honored to be one of the first one hundred paramedics in New Jersey. There have since been about twenty-five thousand paramedics certified in the state. Not bad for a mentally ill person!

I forgot to tell you that one of the examiners on that last station was my savior nurse who'd kept me in the program. We looked right at each other, and I could tell she was more proud of me that day than even I was. I think the fact that she stood by me, with my problems, made her feel pretty good. An empathetic nurse did not discriminate against someone with a mental illness, and a good paramedic was born. This is one of the reasons why I like and respect nurses so much to this day. You will find help along the way—take it!

Deliveries with Love

We responded to routine emergency calls and constant emotional or downright psychologically draining situations, but some were happy occasions. A call came in late one night. A woman in labor needed transport to the hospital. That was routine, and we were always glad to accommodate. Every once in a while, the mother-to-be couldn't make it to the hospital. That was one of those nights. The patient was on the upper floor of an old run-down tenement. When we got into the apartment, it was pitch-dark except for the bluish glow from the

TV. In many of the tenements we responded to, the people were so poor they couldn't afford to replace burned-out light bulbs. The very pregnant lady was lying on the sofa and surrounded by relatives. According to our training, you first determine if it is safe to transport by checking the woman in the vaginal area for crowning. This indicates the birth is imminent. If the baby is crowning, you prepare to deliver the baby right then and there, as lifting and moving the patient would be dangerous at that point. As I checked under the lady's dress for crowning, there suddenly was a commotion. The husband, who was right there, didn't understand what I had to do and thought I was sneaking a peek at his Mrs. I quickly told him why I had to look, but he only spoke Spanish, and by that time his knife was out to defend his wife's honor. Luckily, just at that moment, someone else came into the room who knew English and could translate. He grudgingly set the knife down but didn't put it away.

Our small white obstetrical kit contained sterile latex gloves, drapes to put around the delivery area, ties for the umbilical cord, scissors for cutting the cord, and a bulb aspirator for suctioning fluids from the baby's nose and mouth. I had to get all this stuff ready by the light of the TV. Glad they had a TV because I didn't have a flashlight, and we would have been in total darkness without it. In a few minutes, the baby's head started to peek out, then one shoulder, and then the next. They were the largest parts of the young guy. The rest came fast. The main thing you want when a baby makes its first appearance is to hear a cry or, better yet, a scream. If it's quiet, there is a very good chance that the baby is not breathing. That little one screamed real good! I think he was protesting his exit from his perfectly comfortable location. The husband forgave me and was ecstatic.

The next day we went to see our little guy through the maternity room viewing area. He was still screaming, all swaddled up with his blue knit cap.

That was one of the three deliveries I helped a woman with, and they were all in similar circumstances. It was tremendously satisfying to help a new life into the world, but I felt saddened all three women had to bring their babies into the world while living in poverty and cramped into tiny, dingy tenement apartments with so many people.

By the way, after that night, I always carried a flashlight on calls; no more deliveries by the light of television. Today one of my favorite hobbies is collecting all kinds of flashlights. Every Christmas, I can count on getting at least one flashlight.

4

PTSD (POST-TRAUMATIC STRESS DISORDER)

AS AN EMT AND THEN AS A PARAMEDIC, I RESPONDED to many traumatic calls. The sheer pace, severity, and relentlessness of calls were horrendous. A paramedic's life consists of heart attacks, overdoses, insulin shock, trauma, the responsibility of life or death. There is too much of seeing lives ending too soon or in extreme circumstances, babies that don't wake up, babies being born to a mom with ten others living in a two-bedroom walk-up apartment, constantly being afraid of losing lives if you make a mistake, watching the souls leaving the unlucky ones.

It's an extraordinary business—yes, business. If you can't detach from some of the bad, it possesses you and eats you alive. I was amazed to see myself and fellow first responders perform with superb professionalism when many others would run in the other direction. I rose to the challenges of those chaotic experiences and at times craved even more difficult challenges. You might call it a need for danger or a dopamine rush. My bipolar highs contributed to that craving.

There were horrible calls that imprinted in my memory resulting in lifelong PTSD leading to physically violent nightmares. Other responders might have been more or less affected by them. Many people have experienced traumas in life, way more severe than what I experienced, with no resulting PTSD. Why are some people more likely to develop PTSD than others? I know bipolar makes me more susceptible to stress and was a contributing factor. Many people with bipolar go through traumas dealing with mental illness, mental abuse, and physical abuse. In attending support groups, I notice that most people with bipolar also suffer from PTSD. In my case, I chose a career that guaranteed traumatic experiences. What a dumbass.

Decades after my ambulance career, I still sometimes wake up screaming, violently punching and kicking, trying to save myself from the demons in my night terrors. There is a spectrum of PTSD from mild to severely incapacitating. It can result from being in battle, a victim of crime, abuse, or deprivation or sexual abuse. Witnessing terrible things or sometimes even hearing about them can produce PTSD in some of us. To me PTSD is when dreams and thoughts turn around and become nightmares and demons. I start to dwell on the unbelievability of things that happened in the past. I'm left with hypersensitivity to the stresses that come up in daily life and make me prone to relapsing into bipolar. History reminds me of what I can't forget.

As I was writing this book with the following ambulance calls, my PTSD came back with a vengeance. The horrendous experiences were always on my mind, and I started having violent nightmares again. I had to put writing the book aside. I thought of quitting it altogether. My wife and others encouraged me to continue, so I came up with a plan. I'd finish the stories about the trauma of my illness and most of the emergency responses as rapidly as possible and get them behind me. It worked. It's pretty much a technique I use with PTSD. Acknowledge the past, but don't dwell in it for long. I get up, do chores, go to work, keep busy, go for a long walk, take the dog to the park. It helps to keep to my regular sleep schedule as much as possible, stay on my medicine. I understand the Veterans Administration Hospital system has developed a drug for soldiers that may help others with severe PTSD nightmares. I haven't tried it but thought it was worth mentioning. Probably the most helpful thing is to do something for somebody else. I get away from myself. If the thoughts come back, rinse and repeat. It's only the passage of time that allows the horror to recede to the back of my mind.

I'm sure others would benefit from talk therapy for PTSD; it just wasn't for me. A counselor may help, but I'd rather not talk about my traumatic experiences. It just brings it back and causes more nightmares. For my other bipolar symptoms, talk therapy is effective.

Even with the resulting PTSD, I don't regret my ambulance work. I was always well trained, equipped, and even eager to be there. I am proud of the lives I saved and the comfort I provided to my patients. I never stopped to think about how many tax-paying citizens I brought back, but they probably pay a lot of taxes now. I'm sure their families are mostly glad to have them around too. I was extremely good at preserving people's lives. That was my job. The scars of PTSD are a sign of the wear and tear of a life lived. Life is a piece of art, a painting, sculpture, or a poem. Experiences are changing light and shadows of a life lived and not forgotten.

The following six ambulance calls contributed to my PTSD and may be upsetting due to violence and psychological trauma. If you have doubts about reading these, feel free to skip to the "Lights and Sirens" story.

Boys in the Bridge

I was living with my roommate and partner Willis on the poor side of Elizabeth, when a call way out in the industrial port section of the city came in. It was a long response time of about fifteen minutes. Toward the end of a long straightaway, we could see a cement bridge in the distance. Just off the road to the right, at the bridge's base, was a squished smoking car that had hit the abutment full-on, probably going 90 to 100 mph. The engine was in the front seat with two very dead young boys. There was a weird quietness to their deaths. Those were somebody's sons. The car was smoking, so I told Willis to go back and radio for fire response and another rig. Given the distance from our base and an even longer one to the nearest firehouse, I knew we were on our own.

Amazingly, in the back of the car was a third injured but conscious boy. I was glad we could save one of them. The windows were rolled down, and I asked where he was hurt. As I spoke to him, I noticed empty beer cans were all over the inside and the smell of beer permeated the car. It seemed that youth, beer, and high speed had come together in a bad way.

The front doors of the sedan weren't there anymore. They were both compacted into the car body like accordions from the impact. The car was still smoking. I ran back to the rig and got the longest crowbar we had from the extrication gear. Willis was still on the radio, practically screaming for a fire truck to respond. I told him to come help me, but he was evidently too frightened or panicky to leave the cab of the rig. He was still new to the squad, but there was no excuse.

I got back to the young man and managed to spring the door. I really didn't think I had a chance to do this without the Jaws of Life tool. What a relief when I got the door open wide enough for me to squeeze in. The front of the car was on fire, and there was no time to tend to his injuries. As I tried to get him out of the car, he said he couldn't move. The floorboard had buckled and wedged his foot to the car floor. Things were starting to get hairy. There was no way of knowing if the fire was going to spread to us. It must have been dumb luck, but after a few tries

I twisted his foot to just the right angle to get him free. He would live. As our backup arrived and the fire truck came, Willis was still in the cab even though his main job was to help the patients and me. The fire lieutenant said it looked like the smoke was caused by plumes of steam vapor coming from the ruptured radiator. I would never be able to trust Willis and refused to work or live with him again.

The times when nothing could be done for the patients were hard on us. Often we took it as a personal failure. I couldn't help but think of the suffering the patients might have gone through before they died and all the loved ones they left behind. Death is so final. I still miss the patients who hadn't made it. Even though I didn't know them, they became a part of me.

A lot of us with mental illness have addiction problems with alcohol and drugs. At the time of this accident, I was still binge drinking on nights off. This wasn't the first alcohol-related tragedy I would be called to. It doesn't take a genius to see the common thread. When I saw those boys in the car, my heart sank. The price they paid for a little fun. The effect their deaths would have on their families and friends. Some people never fully bounce back from a loss like that. When you're young, you feel invincible, indestructible, and that bad things won't happen to you. You're not, and they will! It's a matter of time and odds. You may beat the inevitable for a while, but time always wins in the end. Sometimes we may go a little too far with moods of euphoria and invincibility. You've heard it all before, but the obvious takeaway from this call is Don't Drink, Drug Out, and Drive.

The Train

About two in the morning, we responded to where four or five train tracks ran parallel to each other. There were already some cops and detectives milling around one area with flashlights.

They called over for my partner and me. When we got to them, they pointed down to a female torso. They said she had two driver's licenses on her. One put her age at seventeen and the other at twenty-two.

When a lot of us were under twenty-one, we got fake IDs to get into bars and clubs. My guess was that she was walking home after drinking, and as she crossed the multiple lines of tracks, a fast-moving train surprised her. I imagined she only had time to pick one track to stand on with the unimaginable hope the oncoming diesel would not be on that one. If she were drunk, it made it that much harder for her to save herself. I don't think anyone on the scene had ever seen this kind of carnage and trauma happen to a person. The horror of the situation got worse for us. Biff and I were assigned to find the rest of her. As you can imagine, that was a surreal and ghoulish task. It was eerily quiet, and the thought of what we might find bore down on us. It was hot and humid. There was the smell of damp grass and the buzzing of insects. The sickeningly sweet smell of blood and death hung in the air like a ghost.

We found a leg, an arm, another arm, and in some tall grass, her head. As Biff brought her head to be placed by her torso, a detective called out to Biff, "Why don't you dance with her?" I guess people deal with unimaginable tragedy differently. Still, I never forgot what he'd said and find it hard to forgive what it did to my partner and me. It didn't help that we never found one of her legs. Years later, when PTSD returns, I think of that pathetic line. When we returned to base, I got pretty quiet and stayed that way for days. No matter how bad a call was, nobody on the squad got any counseling or time off.

Later that night of the call, Biff was visibly agitated. The agitation continued for a couple of days until one night, sitting alone at a table, he threw his cup of hot tea at the squad room wall and ran out of the room. He never came back to work. Last I heard, he had a breakdown and had stormed into the mayor's office, demanding that the city fix a small sinkhole in his father's yard.

The Barmaid

The call came in as a shooting. Not unusual in our part of town. As a natural result of self-preservation, the police were reluctant to drive around certain areas. I don't blame them. I want to go home to my family after a shift too. Our ambulance squad was instructed not to use lights and sirens in the Port section so we wouldn't attract a crowd. Being that the people didn't like the authorities, that made sense. Until things quieted down, we got in and out as fast as possible.

We got to the street with a row of seedy bars and strip clubs. It was almost like there was a contest to see which one would be the grimmest and most depraved. A couple of anxious customers flagged us down, and we went into the dark abyss. The smell of beer, urine, and vomit instantly made me want to turn and leave. I asked myself, why was I doing this kind of work?

The barmaid was on the floor behind the bar. She had been shot five or six times in her hand, arm, and chest. I imagined her last seconds of terror trying to block the bullets with her hands with no place to run and hide.

I dragged her limp form from behind the bar. She wasn't breathing, there was no pulse, and her young face was ashen. I cut the straps of her clingy, light brown dress to expose her chest for CPR. My partner had forgotten the bag-mask ventilator, so he began mouth-to-mouth breathing. I was concerned for my partner, who had just gotten married, as there was no barrier against fluids and possible diseases. I started chest compressions. The bar floor was filthy and sticky. It was stiflingly hot, and the dank, pungent smells pervaded. Men stood around us and gawked. My imagination was hoping that she would wake up and complain about the dirt on her dress.

We worked to revive her for what seemed like hours but was probably twenty minutes. Doing correct CPR is exhausting and only stops when it is determined that it is futile to continue or the rescuers are too exhausted to sustain it. With the amount of insult her body took, she didn't have much of a chance. In the poverty-stricken neighborhood I worked, it was not uncommon for a boyfriend or husband to go after a woman. It was a harsh and unforgiving environment.

A few days later, I started working with a fellow EMT named Summer. Over a few weeks, I discovered that this cute, petite lady was the best EMT I ever worked with. She could diagnose patients' problems that were not even apparent to emergency-room doctors. One night on the way back from a call, I pointed out the bar where the shooting was. She said before she became an EMT, she was a stripper there. I was impressed that she chose to change the direction of her life from entertainment to saving lives.

Massive Ambulance Response

One Saturday afternoon, there was a regional disaster drill scheduled, including Kennedy, LaGuardia, and especially Newark airports. At high noon we got the call to respond to Newark Airport, the site of the drill. Out of the four ambulances at my station, three left with lights and sirens to participate in the drill, and one stayed back to cover our area of the city in case anything happened. It's always dangerous to be traveling with lights and sirens. There were now about forty rigs from the entire region responding to a simulated airline disaster. There are not many calls that involve so many patients and first responders.

As my crew and I were going through traffic, we thought this would be like a day off, playing make-believe. That changed. We pulled onto the tarmac where the scene of an airline crash was staged. There was a large school bus that represented the plane and near it various people lying on the ground with every imaginable type of injury. The "victims" were primarily made up of Boy Scouts and kids related to the observers. Examiners from the state were watching our every move. As we got closer to the bus, every last kid on the bus was told to scream their heads off to add realism and confusion. On top of that, each "patient" had been decked out in very realistic trauma makeup that you might see in horror movies. There was a doctor-led triage team that went to each victim and placed color-coded tags on them delineating in which order they would be treated. Green for minor injury, yellow for nonthreatening injury, red for life-threatening injury, and black for pain medication until death.

I ended up with four patients. Two had fairly minor injuries and two more severe. One girl had lacerations, burns, and a broken leg. It turned out to be her brother lying next to her. I examined him and asked him where it hurt. He said he couldn't feel his legs. I had to immobilize him for a spinal injury as well as dress burns and cuts. As I was running to the rig for the backboard, the kids we had not gotten off the bus were still yelling. I don't know when it happened, but soon after I arrived in this play-acting, it became absolutely real to me! These kids were really hurt, and some of them were dead or dying. I think that happened to all of us that day. Our training and instinctual desire to preserve life kicked in. As each ambulance crew left with their charges, the realism continued. From all around the city, you could hear dozens of sirens screaming back and forth from the three hospitals.

When we'd finally gotten back to base, I sat on the couch, exhausted. I knew a bipolar depression was setting in. It was time for me to take a couple of weeks off to get back into shape. I was glad I was a sound technician. No one ever questioned my knowledge or competency. I built up a reputation and a reserve that brought me through the tough times, and I knew when to take it easy and step away. If I couldn't do that, I would not do this job.

Later we got feedback from the drill examiners. It turned out that two of my patients were the son and daughter of the doctor who was the regional director of disaster services in charge of the drill and the chief examiners on site. Everyone on my ambulance squad passed.

Airline Disaster

I didn't know it at the time, but years later the disaster we practiced for was going to happen for real. I would no longer be a paramedic but a Red Cross volunteer on a disaster action team.

It was a stormy, windy night in July when a DC-9 with fifty-seven people aboard made its final approach a half mile from touchdown at Charlotte Douglas Airport. As it flew very low into a thunderstorm, a microburst produced an overwhelming wind shear that slammed the airliner into the ground. I was on call with a disaster team when the call came from first responders that there were some survivors and to bring blankets for them.

When we arrived, we could see the plane had crashed into a wooded neighborhood, partially resting on a street. It was in four pieces, one of which had hit a house. Two massive yellow airport fire trucks had put the fires out, but there was still jet fuel all over, and the thick smell of kerosene permeated the air.

By the time we got there, all the survivors had been transported to hospitals and those who had not survived were covered with tarps. Amazingly there were twenty survivors, some with critical burns, some with lacerations and broken bones, and a few who could walk away without a scratch. The house was unoccupied. Survival can be so arbitrary. We set up our station inside the crime-scene tape that surrounded the plane about thirty feet from the cockpit section. We started handing out drinks and snacks to the first responders. One of the firemen said part of the fuselage went into a house that had a lot of children in it. When there was a lull in our duties, I noticed a large blue tarp not more than twenty feet from us. They said that's where they placed the children. The brokenhearted responders wanted them to be together. I couldn't take my eyes off it. I was weeping inside for the little ones under the blue tarp. I still think of them today, and whenever I see a blue tarp, I feel sad.

As we continued giving out drinks, I couldn't help but notice how quiet it was. It wasn't at all noisy and confusing like the airline disaster drill I was at years earlier.

A fireman said to me, "Be sure to look up in the trees."

I said, "For what?"

"Bodies," he said.

With the impact, people could have been thrown into the trees. The scene of the tragedy was now lit up with banks of powerful floodlights so the responders could do their work. The lights cast crooked shadows among the trees. The smells, the incredible sight of a large plane sticking out of the house, the cockpit on the street, and the fact that so many lost their lives there was overwhelming. As the light flickered eerily through the trees, I imagined a poor soul would fall from a tree and land on me, or a horribly injured passenger would appear from behind a tree, begging for help. I have never been in such a surreal, ghastly, mind-bending situation.

The next day I realized I had not even given aid to a single victim or saw one dead body as all the victims had already been taken to hospitals, and all the bodies were under tarps. Even so, that call lingers as a constant source of PTSD pain. I can't watch airline crashes on the news, but strangely enough, if an airline crash occurred near me today, I would be drawn to the location to help.

The Darkest Night—The Darkest Call

I didn't want to put this call in the book. It's the hardest one for me to think and write about. I left it out of the original manuscript but decided to put it in. I wanted to face this PTSD once and for all. Talk therapy didn't help, but writing about it did.

It was another of those August three a.m. calls. It was oppressively hot and so humid our uniforms stuck to us even before we left base. I was working my regular eleven p.m. to seven a.m. shift. That night I was going to find out why they call it the graveyard shift. George and I had just spent about an hour with a heart attack victim. The patient was a big guy with a massive barrel chest, weighing in at over 250 lbs. He lived on the third floor of a walk-up apartment building. When we got there, he was in cardiac arrest. We immediately started CPR. Being EMTs in the mid-seventies, we didn't have access to advance life-support protocols. Our training allowed us to do CPR, administer oxygen, and transport as rapidly as possible. Our job was to get this guy down three flights of stairs while continuing compressions and breathing. At that period of time in our city, police and fire departments rarely responded with us. If we stopped for very long or did ineffective CPR, this fellow could suffer permanent brain damage from lack of oxygen to his brain. This wasn't George's and my first rodeo. We had done many similar rescues.

We got him on the stretcher and lashed him in securely, barely stopping our compressions. We moved down each flight of stairs, stopped on the landing, and continued CPR. He was dead weight; technically he was dead. We had to lift him up almost vertically to get around the bends in the staircases. He soon started to feel as heavy as a piano as we strained every muscle and ounce of strength to accomplish our mission. If you have ever done CPR for fifteen or twenty minutes, you know that it is exhausting. Now do it down three flights of stairs and then some more in the back of a moving ambulance.

En route to the hospital, we got another call on the radio. Can you guess the nature of the next call? It just had to be another heart attack. We dropped off our patient and went speeding, lights and sirens, toward a new location. My arms were so tired I could hardly grip the steering wheel, and George could only sit slumped down in the seat. I should mention that the air conditioners on the rigs never worked. I guess the city hadn't budgeted for repairs to the entire ambulance fleet or just couldn't take them out of service long enough for repairs. It was absolutely stifling to the point we could hardly breath.

When we got to the new patient's building, we were soaked in our own sweat and then swam through the soupy air from the sidewalk to the foyer. When we got to the gentleman's apartment, he was conscious but having great difficulty breathing. After a quick interview and history, we determined that he had congestive heart failure and was deteriorating fast. He reminded me of my father, around the same age and build, and he seemed like a nice man. His breathing became alarmingly labored. George went back to the rig and got the cardiac chair. That's a portable chair used to take patients to the ambulance without laying them down. We didn't dare lay him down because that would have made his breathing worse. The chair had four handles on it, so we carried him, sitting in the chair, down the steps to the outside of the building.

As I looked toward my rig, all emergency flashing lights and the floodlights were dark. It was standard procedure to leave the lights on. That had never happened before. It got worse, much worse. We got the patient secured to the inside of the rig. I went to start it—and nothing. It didn't even turn over. I could hear the patient getting worse in the back. The radio was absolutely dead, and when I tried the walkie-talkie, we were out of range. It was around four in the morning, there was no one on the street, no cars, no building lights, nothing. It was like being in a deep canyon made up of tall buildings with walls too steep to climb and with no hope of rescue. As I said, George and I were completely and utterly spent, and George had thrown up. We could hardly stand and were helpless. Our poor man was gurgling now. His heart was failing, and fluids were rapidly building up in his lungs. He was drowning in his own backed-up fluids.

We could only sit and listen to another human die. That was not the way it was supposed to be. We were only seven minutes from the hospital. A tragic series of events took the last chance of life from this man. An old broken-down ambulance, no working radio, a walkie-talkie out of range—cell phones hadn't been invented yet—a dark and deserted cityscape with two exhausted rescuers. I doubt if further treatment would have saved him, but we were helpless and had no control. I prided myself on keeping my patients alive to reach the hospital. I felt I died that night with him. It truly was the graveyard shift. I think of this man almost every day.

Lights and Sirens

The call came in as a heart attack, which is where we can consistently make a difference in someone's life. Obviously, the sooner we get to the patient, the better the outcome. We move more rapidly for these situations. Believe it or not, we are told not to exceed the posted speed limit. Fat chance! We were dodging in and out of traffic, with lights and sirens going. Out of nowhere, a car cut in front of us and almost stopped. It was the only time I came that close to a crash. I couldn't believe it when a few days later I found out an ex-girlfriend was in the car that cut us off. What a small town the big city was.

We still got to the location in record time. It was a single-family house, and an elderly lady answered the door. We asked her to show us where the patient was. She led us to the kitchen, where her husband was sitting at the table, eating a sandwich. He didn't look to be in any distress. The lady turned to us and said, "Would you tell my husband to turn the thermostat up? I'm cold, and no matter how many times I turn it up, he turns it down again."

It was a relief the gentleman was okay, but my partner and I still had a lot of adrenaline pumping. We managed to tell them that calling Emergency Medical Services for a nonemergency is against the law, and please don't do it again, or we would have them arrested. We walked them over to the thermostat and arrived at an agreeable temperature setting. On the way back to base, we took it slow and tried to relax before the next call came in.

We got back to the station. Like a fireman or a soldier, there are times of boredom. Some nights we would be running from one call to another and occasionally have a call backed up. Nights on the graveyard shift were always the busiest and most violent. That's when most bad things happen. At arbitrary times things would go quiet, too quiet. It would never last. A sweltering summer night would put people into the streets. Heat makes people irritable, driving them to make poor decisions. Alcohol and drugs among a population with little hope and nothing to lose are the ingredients for chaos.

What a lucky break for my partner and me when we were assigned a routine transport call. We were to take a young man suffering from psychosis to the state mental hospital in the southern part of the state. The three-hour round trip out of town at a leisurely pace was like a mini vacation away from the sizzling city.

Off we went. I was in the back with the patient, talking and trying to reassure and comfort him in in what was probably the most difficult and bewildering time in his young life. There are so many times when emergency workers provide meaningful comfort and reassurance to those under their care. I couldn't help but think back to not very long ago when I was in his position. In an unbelievable coincidence, the hospital we took him to was the same one I was admitted to after my first breakdown. It's hard to say how I felt as we waited in admitting with our patient. I had the feeling that things had come full circle for me. I was grateful that my life had changed enough to be the caregiver and not the one being cared for.

After the young man was admitted, it was time to return to base. I don't know what possessed me. Perhaps I was celebrating my successful recovery years ago when I was discharged from the same hospital. As soon as we got off the hospital grounds, I activated all the switches on the ambulance console to full lights and sirens. I told my startled partner we were going to run like this for the entire hour-and-a-half trip back. He just smiled and said he was game. We both knew we would be fired if we were discovered. Still, the heat of summer combined with one crappy call after another in the city gave us both the unspoken understanding that being fired might be better than doing this insane work. We didn't care anymore. We were living in a job that surrounded us with heartache and death. It felt exhilarating and free, driving away in our screaming ambulance with the windows wide open, speeding away from the hospital that had once captured me in its horror.

We traveled through one small town after another since there was no direct route from the hospital to base. We were extra cautious of pedestrians and traffic, proceeding slowly through intersections. We were morons, but not complete irresponsible jerks. At one point along the way, a patrol car pulled alongside us. I hadn't thought the police would bother us, and that could have been an abrupt end to our joyride. We didn't have radio communication with the cop, but he gave us a long fish eye. If we shut down our lights and sirens, he would know what was up. And if he was having a bad day or was a rookie, we would have been at his mercy. He could see by the big letters on our rig that we weren't a local squad, but luckily, he didn't stop us. I guess he figured we had a reason to get back to the city in a hurry. We shut everything down when we hit our city limits. It was ironic that our escapade brought us back a half hour earlier than expected. Back into the cauldron!

Ten Thousand is Too Much

The average EMT burns out in ten years. The job doesn't lend itself to long careers. I worked in a particularly harsh inner-city environment with all the illness, suffering, violence, and psychological trauma that ambulance work brought. I had also worked as an EMT emergency room technician in a hospital in Elizabeth and also volunteered in the emergency room at the Medical College Hospital in Newark, NJ, in my spare time. It was the Wild West in Newark emergency care. At the time, Newark was the murder capital of New Jersey, and with Jersey's reputation, that's saying something.

The physical demands of the job are significant. You may have to lift a patient weighing about 275 plus the weight of the stretcher and an oxygen tank. At times I felt like an ant that can lift more than its own body weight. You're in and out of precarious positions and situations. Still, the patient always comes first, and the rescuers end up with lots of bumps, cuts, bruises, and long-term injuries that can last a lifetime. In my case, it was worn-out hips from lifting, hearing loss from the sirens, and PTSD. Training dictates the rescuer must come first and not to put themselves in harm's way and become another patient needing rescue, but most of us put the patient first and did what we had to do despite the training. My little joyride coming back from the hospital let me know I no longer cared as much as I used to about keeping the job.

The nagging bouts of bipolar were always there. I was in partial remission, but it took a lot out of me to be constantly on guard against the illness. The best I could do was stay on my meds and talk things over with my shrinks. I was tired of holding it together for my patients at the expense of myself. I knew it was time to quit when I was no longer able to detach from the patients. Something had to give.

We had many repeat patients. One call would come in as a mugging with a stabbing. When we would get there, it was the same guy we had seen many times. He take a knife under a bridge and make numerous deep cuts in both arms. He would then appear above the bridge and claim he had been mugged and stabbed. He did this at least nine or ten times when I was on duty and no telling how many on other shifts. We bandaged him and took him to the ER, where they stitched him up again and sent him on his way. Apparently, nobody at the hospital reached out to help him even though they knew him and his cutting problem very well. We didn't have the authority to refer someone for mental help, let alone take them for the real treatment that they desperately needed. There were too many repetitive calls where I could not do anything of real value. It was incredibly frustrating.

I had a young patient about fourteen years old, but it's hard to tell how old a dying child is. We were always going to his house to transport him to the hospital. He didn't weigh anything. Since I met him, all he could do was lie on his parents' sofa swaddled up like a baby. He had leukemia and was so frail, so thin, and so pale. The months passed, and we took him back and forth from the hospital. We always talked in the back of the ambulance, but he never complained; he only showed resignation to his situation. On one of these rides he told me he wanted to die at home. One day we went to his house to transport him to the hospital, but when we got there, he had died. It still hit me hard even though I knew he was dying. We spent our last time together in the ambulance, and I started obsessing about how lonely he must be now after he was dead and away from his parents.

My professionalism was turning into heartbreak. The effects of post-traumatic stress disorder were continuing to take its toll. The many bad calls combined with the accumulation of thousands of other calls got to the point it wasn't working for me anymore. I no longer let myself get close to my patients. If I couldn't save or make a difference for them, I hated it. When I started feeling that I couldn't control enough outcomes, I felt useless. Even though out of thousands of calls with very few who died before we were able to get to the hospital, I still started blaming myself for things completely out of my control. I started dwelling on the kids, especially crib deaths. I wanted to be able to save everyone. I really felt the spirit of the babies in the room who died in their crib and wanted to be able to make them breathe again. I'm not a control freak, but I didn't like it one bit. I just couldn't handle it anymore. I had said to myself if that ever happened to me, I would get out. It wouldn't be good for the patient, and it would destroy me. Close to ten years and over ten thousand calls were too much. This was the end of what I lived and put my life at risk for. It was over!

THIS IS HOW IT'S SUPPOSED TO BE...
MOSTLY

MY WIFE AND I HAD ALMOST TWENTY YEARS WHERE there were mostly only minor ups and downs. With few exceptions, there was nothing near the intolerable debilitating mood swings of destructive manic highs or deep depressive lows. Despite mental illness, we started having an almost model life. We were involved with our church, scouting, family, and friends. We raised a fantastic son who is bipolar-free. He is an Eagle Scout and a college graduate with a successful career who would be embarrassed if I told you of his talents and successes. He owns a house with a wonderful woman whom we both love.

Mary

You often hear "The woman behind the man." In my case, the woman is why there is a man! I was always working weekends on the ambulance, so I didn't have that great of a social life. I was feeling burned out from ambulance work, and to have some fun and meet girls, I would go to Sneaky Pete's, a bar and dance club a few towns away. They always had a great live band. Every Saturday night, I would go up there before work and have a beer. Just one, mind you! It was a fun place, and we were all immortals in our twenties. During all the times at Sneaky Pete's, I had danced with a few girls but never dated anyone. That all changed when I saw Mary across the room. We all know how it goes from there.

This tall, slender girl with straight, waist-long, blond hair instantly captivated me. She was a California beauty right smack in the middle of New Jersey. I had never been to California, but I thought I knew what it was like because I listened to the music of the Beach Boys. I didn't hesitate in the least and went right over and asked her to dance, which was unusual for me. We danced to some rock music, but when they started playing a slow ballad, we went off the dance floor to talk. It was still loud in the club, so we went outside, and she sat on the hood of my car. If this girl had a personality, we might have something. She did, in spades! We talked and talked and smoked our Marlboros. An hour passed and then another, and it was getting time for me to leave for work. That one beer had worn off long ago. Mary was a Navy brat when she was young. Her family was stationed in various places, including the naval base in Norfolk, Virginia, where she was born. She also spent some time growing up close to the naval base in San Diego. She really was a California girl!

We started dating and didn't go another day without seeing each other until the day before our wedding about thirteen months later. We talked about my being bipolar before we were married but she married me anyway. Still, having not seen me depressed or manic, she really didn't know what she was getting into. We had a big reception under a giant tent on Long Island. I'll never forget when one of my brothers was giving the best man toast started his little speech with "Growing up with John has been an interesting experience." I think that sums up my formative years.

At one point, I asked Mary what she liked about me. She said she always wanted to be an EMT, so I intrigued her and that I cared about people and was nice to everyone. So being an EMT paid off. In fact, she soon got her EMT certification. She never officially worked in the profession, but being a certified EMT is something we now had in common.

I could go on and on about my Mary. She wouldn't want me to do that. Anyone who can stay with the typical bipolar for decades must have an extraordinary ability to love, share, and have patience and understanding. Most women would have given up on me. Luckily, I am a prince in deep disguise. At a time when I was done with ambulance work, Mary supported my going back to school to get my Bachelor of Science degree in Allied Health. Over the years, she supported my many career changes: education for a certificate in graphic arts, warehouse worker, dental lab technician, Realtors license, numerous recertifications, volunteer work, and way too many silly endeavors through the years. I made some rescues, but Mary rescued this rescuer time and again.

Why would this bright, beautiful woman stay with a man like me? She was not a woman but a bulldog, and she would never give up on me. This tenacity runs through her like a vein of gold and is one of the reasons she is so successful in everything she does. If you find someone who does half of what my wife does and puts up with you, well, you know what to do!

The Rockies

My career in paramedicine ended, and Mary and I moved to Colorado. After a few years, we bought our first home, a little two-bedroom mountain house at 8,300-feet elevation in the front range of the Rockies outside of Denver. In the winter, the view outside our windows made us feel we were living inside a Currier and Ives Christmas scene.

I sold real estate for a living. Driving the winding mountain roads proved interesting where switchbacks and steep hills are typical. There were plenty of elk and deer that seemed to like to test unsuspecting driver skills. Adding in the snow and ice, getting around safely was challenging.

During my time living in the mountains, I ended up stopping for several serious accidents. One involved a camper shell that flew off a pickup onto the opposite side of the highway into the windshield of an oncoming car. We had to call in the flight for life helicopter from Denver General Hospital for two of these incidents. I wasn't working as a paramedic, but I was always on the lookout to help. I really missed helping people and making an immediate impact in their lives. It is hard to get the adventure and feeling of fulfillment of ambulance work out of your blood. I thought I might as well get my EMT recertification. It came in handy, but I never worked professionally again.

We started to consider having a baby. We talked about whether we should or not because of the concern about the baby developing bipolar. We spoke to our family doctor and my psychiatrist. They were reluctant to give such personal opinions but did present us with some facts. There is a hereditary factor to bipolar, so it was a worry our baby would develop it too. The doctors at the time thought it would be about one in five odds of our child having bipolar. We decided we could live with those odds, and if our baby developed bipolar, we could live with that too. There were worse things.

It wasn't long before the pitter patter of little feet would arrive. My wife had a long labor. I'm glad we had decided to deliver at the hospital and not with our local family doctor because there was a serious complication at our son's birth. I was in the delivery room. With nerves of steel, I kept dropping our newly purchased 35mm camera loaded with low light film so we would not need a flash to record the moment of our baby's arrival. My wife told me to put the damn thing away. When the baby came, he wasn't crying. You always want to hear that screaming. Screaming equals breathing. He was breathing slightly but was very blue and not pinking up. The doctor quickly had me cut the cord and handed our limp infant to the nurse, who suctioned out his nose and mouth. He started to cry a little bit. The doctor let my wife hold him for a few seconds and then scooped him up and disappeared out of the room to the neonatal intensive care. We were stunned; this wasn't the way it was supposed to be.

My wife was moved back to her room, where we were told the baby was born with inadequate tissue profusion. They explained his blood was not circulating well enough to keep him alive. By sheer luck, one of the most preeminent neonatal doctors in the region happened to be attending one of his other patients on our son's floor. It was two a.m.; he came into my wife's room. Was it going to be good news or bad? He wanted our immediate permission to give the baby a blood transfusion. That was the time when the HIV/AIDs epidemic was at its peak. Tests had not yet been developed to verify that blood in the blood bank was HIV-free. There was no real treatment or cure. Many were contracting it and dying. Our decision came down to saving the baby now or possibly giving him a slow death later. Many people at the time would not even consider a blood transfusion.

We went forward with the blood transfusion, and our baby responded well and recovered nicely. Five days later, a nurse was walking my wife and me to the main lobby of the hospital. My wife was carrying a bright pink little boy in her arms. When we got to the doors of the hospital, security stopped us. I couldn't imagine what the problem was. It was October, and a snowstorm in the mountains had turned into a blizzard. The highway department was going to close the pass near our house because it looked like it would soon become impassible. Again, this wasn't the way it was supposed to be. They wouldn't let us try to get home without the doctor's permission. We sent the nurse upstairs to plead with the doctor. When she got back, she had a gigantic smile on her face and wished our new family farewell and good luck. Well, they closed the pass soon after we went through, and the blizzard snowed us in for two days. What did it matter?

All sorts of relatives visited our new baby. My wife's parents came right away and helped out a lot. They were followed by my mom and sister. It was the first time they visited us. The fact that our house was at 8,300 feet and the fact that they were both smokers meant that they soon had the uncomfortable feeling of being short of breath. There isn't much oxygen at that level. After they got back home, they let us know that they wouldn't be able to visit again. One of my brothers and his wife visited from Leadville, CO, the highest city in North America. They were used to the altitude.

I was amazed and grateful that with all the stress and change of a new baby, I had no symptoms of bipolar. I was so glad to feel "normal" and that we had decided to have a baby! Our wedding song was "We've Only Just Begun" by the Carpenters. It was a new beginning. Oh, how much I loved my wife and baby. We were having a wonderful life.

After about a year, we started to realize that there wouldn't be much to do for our little boy in our current location. There was no daycare to speak of, no little league or scouts. There was a local elementary school, but the middle and high school would be a long bus ride away. My wife was commuting to Denver by way of the only highway out of the mountains. It was a winding two-lane road that was notoriously unsafe to drive and, in the winter, downright dangerous. After a snowfall, on the way down you would pass one turned-over car after another. Those were mostly four-wheel-drive SUVs that learned the hard way. Four-wheel drive doesn't help on ice. Most of the time, no one went over a cliff, but truck drivers who didn't know the area weren't always so lucky. The road was so bad that a lot of cars had a bumper sticker that read "Pray for me, I drive Highway 285." One thing I learned from real estate is the first priority where to live is location, location, location. Spending hours shoveling snow got old. Would you believe we had to dig down in the snow to get to the woodpile, which was stacked at over six feet? The stars were lining up. We would move back east where we thought our son would have more opportunities and his relatives could breathe.

Schizophrenic Again

After moving to North Carolina, I earned my new real estate license, and things were going very well, mood-wise. I hadn't had a breakdown or significant mood swing in many years. A record! I wanted to try to get off my meds and continue healthy living with exercise and good food without all the extra drug chemistry. My wife and I talked about it and decided to go for it and stop the meds. I stopped taking them, and within a week or so, I was starting to get hyper. Talking fast, racing thoughts, staying up late, and not sleeping well. It wasn't long till I thought everything on TV was just for me and totally relevant to me. If there was an exercise program on, I thought the exercise program was designed just for me because I needed more exercise. I was overly concerned with myself, getting paranoid thinking everyone was talking about me even though they could not have cared less. I didn't recognize the next-door neighbor.

It hadn't occurred to me that before I started my little experiment, I should establish a relationship with a local psychiatrist. I hadn't done that. What a dumbass. I went to a family doctor, and he referred us to a shrink. The new psychiatrist was the head of the psychiatric floor at one of the biggest hospitals in the area. A big-wig.

By the time my wife brought me to his office, I was pretty much out of my mind. I had a total and complete relapse of the worst my bipolar could offer. The doctor took me to an exam room where he tried to talk to me and gave me verbal tests. Not knowing my history, he determined I was schizophrenic as I could not respond appropriately. He wanted to put me on powerful drugs to treat schizophrenia and had my wife sign permission papers to start this drug therapy. I was too far gone to know any better and fill him in on my history, so treatment was started. He could have admitted me to the hospital but thought my wife could take care of me.

The meds helped a little, but I did not improve much with that regime. So after a few weeks, my wife found another psychiatrist. I was able to hold it together long enough to have a long talk with the new doctor. He said, in no uncertain terms, that I was not schizophrenic but bipolar. It was not surprising the medications for schizophrenia didn't work well; they were the wrong medicines. It would have been nice if he said I just had some minor problems and I'd be better in no time. Dream on! He started me on appropriate drugs that stabilized me. I began getting much better, and I avoided having to be admitted to the hospital.

I'm sure I presented to the first doctor with schizophrenic-like symptoms, but if he had taken a good history of my illness and observed me over time, he would have realized I was bipolar. With the right diagnosis and medications, I could have recovered sooner. The longer symptoms last, the harder it is to bounce back, which takes a tremendous emotional toll on you and your loved ones. My wife had never seen me with so many distinct, disturbing symptoms. She tried to talk to me and reassure me that I would eventually feel like myself again. She spent a lot of time trying to ground me back to reality. What was real, and what was in my disturbed mind? She was working full time and tried to talk to me from work, but it was difficult as we had decided not to tell people due to possible discrimination. There were multiple times she left work early to come home to "talk me down." She wasn't sleeping either due to the stress at work, taking care of our one-year-old, and taking care of a mentally ill person. This really takes a toll on a marriage. I felt especially bad as a man, who is viewed as the provider and protector, that I had to be taken care of by my wife. It was hard on my ego. It was also emotionally and physically draining on my wife. It takes work and devotion to stay committed to each other. I'm glad my wife has the tenacity of a bulldog; she doesn't give up. Being extra caring to your spouse between episodes does not hurt either.

There are many takeaways here. Don't stop taking your meds without first having expert guidance. If the doctor is not a good fit, or you think you need a second opinion, find another doctor. Don't be discouraged if you have a relapse, because you will get through it.

One Shot to the Head

I saw my new psychiatrist often and always liked seeing him. He was married, about fifty with white hair, a kind face, and very knowledgeable. I saw him often and always felt he was helping me. I told him how unhappy I was being bipolar and that I would again like to stop taking my meds. At the time, I was working in a cold, drafty warehouse, where I was one of the few workers who spoke English. He asked me if I had any hobbies and what I did for fun. I said I hung around the house most of the time, playing with the dog in the backyard and watching too much TV. He shared with me that he enjoyed playing chess and had an extensive gun collection. As the months passed, I was steadily improving but still hated my warehouse job and was depressed.

At my last appointment with him, we went over some of my latest problems and concerns. Toward the end of the visit, he started giving me concrete advice on what to do with my life. He told me not to quit my job and not to stop taking my meds. He never gave me such concrete advice before. Having seen many psychiatrists in the past, I knew that they rarely come out and tell you what to do or not to do. A few days before my next appointment, my wife's life was threatened by someone she had a part in firing. Of course, this was a significant stressor, so I called my psychiatrist's office for an appointment. The receptionist said, "I'm sorry, but the doctor has taken his own life." That wasn't the way it was supposed to be.

A few days later, his office called me and said they were offering a group counseling meeting for his patients. I didn't go but should have. I still feel guilty that I burdened him with my troubles. Where were the counseling sessions for my doctor when he was in trouble? Going back to my last visit with him, I could see the change in him from a professional to someone who just wanted things to work out for me. He told me not to quit my job and keep taking my meds. I asked his secretary how he killed himself. He shot himself in the head. He was bipolar as well. I loved this man and his kind face and will miss him forever.

This brought back a childhood memory of my first experience with suicide. I was staying at my Aunt Ruth's house. It was Christmas day, and I was five or six. Dad was in a mental hospital for the holidays, and my older brother and I were at my aunt's house so my mom could visit my dad. It was a warm day for December, so after we opened our presents, I went outside. On the curb, at the next-door neighbor's house, I saw a Christmas tree. I thought how strange because Christmas was still going on. When I looked closer, I could see it still had on all its lights, decorations, and tinsel. I couldn't believe my luck. I started retrieving the lights and some bright balls. As I pulled on a set of lights, I dislodged the tree from the rest of the trash. The rest of the trash turned out to be a mattress saturated with thick, gooey blood. This wasn't nosebleed blood like I had seen before. On Christmas Eve, the young man who lived with his parents had asked his longtime girlfriend to marry him. She had said no. That Christmas, a shotgun put a young man's brains on the walls of his room. At that point in my life, the innocence of childhood had never let me consider that someone would want to end his life. I thought, how could life get so hard, and would it ever get that hard for me?

The incidence of suicide among people with bipolar is up to a startling twenty percent. If a skilled and experienced doctor gives up, how are we expected to cope any better? My doctor, like most dedicated doctors, took on the pain of his patients. By being there with his patients, he was extraordinarily empathetic and very effective. When you can't leave your patient's pain behind, and you have so much of your own besides, there can be a tragic result if you don't get help. It reminded me of why I left paramedicine when the patients' burdens got to be too much for me. Most of us with garden-variety bipolar don't have to deal with what a troubled clinician does. Suicide is still an ever-present danger for us. If you ever find yourself there, talk to someone even if it is hard. There are hotlines available twenty-four hours a day.

National Suicide Prevention Lifeline

1-800-273-8255

Available twenty-four hours a day, seven days a week.

She's Not in the Creek

After my doctor's suicide, I found another psychiatrist who kept me well stabilized with my medications. I also started seeing a psychologist counselor who helped me get over the sadness and guilt of losing him. This combination of a psychiatrist to keep me stable and the right medications did help. Except for PTSD, a counselor for talk therapy has always worked well for me as well. It was such a relief to have this support in place again.

Over time I had of series of jobs. I earned a certificate in graphic arts and did some industrial photography, but most were boring, low paying, and unsatisfying. I missed the excitement and satisfaction of rescuing people.

At times, I was able to make contributions in my everyday life. It was a standard Saturday afternoon when there was a commotion outside. Down the street, there were a lot of police cars in front of a house. Being my curious self, I walked down to see what was going on. A little girl in first grade had disappeared. Evidently, her school gave the kids candy bars to sell around the neighborhood to raise money for who knows what. The girl was selling candy earlier in the neighborhood with her mother. It seemed the little girl was quite an entrepreneur, and she slipped out of the house unnoticed by her mom. Mom looked all over for her daughter, but she was nowhere to be found. The police and some other neighbors had just started looking for this little girl.

Thinking about our area, it occurred to me there was a creek about a quarter-mile downhill from the lost girl's house. I had gone down there many times because it reminded me of when I was kid looking for tadpoles, frogs, and fish. It was a good place to just get away and relax. Through the years, I had seen numerous news reports of kids who turned up missing and had drowned in creeks. I just had a feeling. I hopped in my car and got to the creek. I was more than grateful not to find her at or especially in the creek. I got back in the car, and a few blocks from the creek, there she was, walking up to a stranger's house, hawking those damn candy bars. I accompanied her to the door and asked the lady who answered if we could use her phone. The cops would have found her eventually, but I felt that old feeling of being able to rescue come back. It motivated me to start volunteering at the Red Cross again.

It had been a long time since I had done anything productive. I was pretty much sitting around the house, not working. For me, in a strange way, what happened with the lost girl was almost fun. Because of my past rescue work, I had come to miss the satisfaction of it. I think most of us who do good things, deep down, really do them for ourselves. We get nice feelings and maybe even a sort of high from good deeds. My belief is that as civilians, we are all brothers and sisters and want to get that feeling of doing the right thing for others.

Trying Not to be a Dumbass

Although there were not huge mood swings, there were many times my mania took control, and it felt good to be a dumbass. No one knew I was bipolar; they just thought I was a jerk. Bipolar is my excuse, and I'm sticking to it! My wife and I argued about my manic behavior many times. It put my wife in a position to cover for me and help me with my over-the-top manic behavior. It is not the best dynamic in a marriage. She knew I was triggered by the overstimulation of a family gathering, but that didn't make it any easier for us.

Over-the-top joking and fooling around at the Thanksgiving table gets applause and laughs from the kids but not from the adults. When they were young, my nieces and nephews were laughing at my "marvelous" routines and jokes while I ignored my wife kicking me under the table and giving me "the look." Many Thanksgivings passed before I could calm down and maybe even grow up a little and try harder to be acceptable. I learned to step away when I was getting too wound up, if only for a couple of minutes. This gives me a breather and helps me to reset.

Being a dumbass is fun until the inevitable depression sets in. I might be going along fine one day and be stable, and then the next day I would feel different. It would be like giving a kid a new bike and then taking it away without saying why. There was hardly ever a reason for my depressive phases; I just attributed them to changes in my brain chemistry due to bipolar.

My wife said she'd seen it coming for over two weeks. It's a familiar pattern for me; mild mania, critical, spewing crude and useless comments about what was on TV, not sleeping, and then descending into depression. When I'm depressed and irritable, it's probably best if I just surf the net rather than veg out on the networks, spewing my critical comments at the TV. At least we don't pay for cable, so there are not a hundred more channels to curse. To tell you the truth, I'm extremely tired of these cycles. If it wasn't for mild mania and "normal" times, I think I would have checked out a long time ago. You could say, "This is the hand you're dealt with, deal with it." I think I said that you should accept responsibility for your illness. Today I should listen to my own frigging advice!

When in the middle of a depression, it is hard to remember what helps and even harder to do it. It's important to keep a record through the years on what is successful. The depression cure for me, if you can call it that, is to keep busy, try to move and get walking, eat well, keep my sleep schedule by not sleeping too much, stay in touch with people, take my meds, talk to my counselor, or get a temporary med adjustment. It can take weeks or months, but over time I always start to feel better and may even get a bit hyper again. I'd much rather be on the mildly manic part of the mood scale but have learned to be careful as it can slip into full-blown mania.

It comes back to happiness. Everyone wants it but feels we don't have enough of it or none at all. Don't be a dumbass. It's right there in front of you. It's the life you have been given. Maybe you won't be president, although history has produced some mentally unsound presidents. What the hell, do *something*. Does it matter what? Who are you trying to impress? If you want to impress someone, impress yourself, do something good, help someone, or better yet, help yourself so you'll be able to make a difference in your own or someone else's life. Have fun doing it, and maybe others will come to the party.

The Towers

Sometimes mild depression, a manic episode, or a new experience causes me to overthink the past and triggers PTSD.

My wife and I had a long history with the Trade Center. We were engaged at Windows on the World, the restaurant on the 107th floor of one of the towers at the World Trade Center. My wife's commute included crossing under the river by train from New Jersey to the station in the basement of the Trade Center. She would take the escalator to street level and walk the rest of the way to work. Before we moved to North Carolina, we'd visit New York to see Broadway shows and often went up to the observation area in the Center while we were in town. Of course, the view from the top of the Trade Center was magnificent. I couldn't help but think of the native American name "Manahactanienk," meaning place of inebriation. I imagined what those long-ago natives of the city would say; the white man must have been drunk to build their lodges so close together.

I was watching TV when the war started. One tower was burning, and then the second tower was hit. There was lots of paper and debris coming from the buildings. It soon became horribly apparent that some of what was falling from the towers were people. Cameramen were recording images of our neighbors leaping to their deaths rather than suffer the excruciating agony of burning to death. It felt so personal. If things were different, my wife could have been there. She told me she couldn't get the faces of the people who'd shared the space with her on their way to work every day out of her mind. She knew some of them were there that day and worried about the homeless man she'd pass at the base of the tower. I, too, couldn't shake the thoughts of watching live TV of innocent people meeting such an unimaginably violent death. I can't even imagine what the people actually there and the first responders had to go through and the memories they would be left with.

Do you remember back, soon after those videos started appearing on the news, they were discontinued and not shown to the public anymore? This was because the images were giving thousands of us a form of PTSD. Everyone at the restaurant was killed. This was Manhattan, New York, an edifice of the country, and now the Pearl Harbor of our generation. It was also a place where young lovers made a promise. That was not how it was supposed to be.

Years later, I volunteered for a research study about bipolar disorder. One part of the study consisted of observing my brain activity using MRI, Magnetic Resonance Imaging. They can see changes in blood flow and neurological brain activity. While I was in the machine, scientists would flash different images on a monitor as I watched. The reason I mention this study is because one thing stood out in all the testing and observing. I was shown lots of different pictures and video footage. The scientists were studying my brain and how it reacted. They could literally see parts of my brain light up with activity in various regions. I watched lots of different things. Suddenly at one point, they showed me the horribly disturbing videos of men and women jumping to their deaths at the Trade Center. They were the only images that they showed me over and over again. My brain activity must have lit up.

The videos were hard to watch, and I don't think the scientists were sadists. The only reason I can think they did that was to study the effects these kinds of images have on the brain. I assume it had to do with studying PTSD. It had been documented that 10,000 people suffered diagnosable PTSD symptoms from the news coverage. They wouldn't give me any results of the tests, but I got a big thank-you and one hundred dollars.

Discrimination

Until very recently, I had only told the immediate family that I am bipolar. Mary and I decided not even to tell our son until he was a teenager. You could say that in some sense I'm coming out now. In the more than fifty years with the illness, I have told members of the National Alliance on Mental Illness (NAMI) and support groups, but I don't even tell many of my doctors. It's not news that there is a stigma to mental illness. Discrimination comes in many forms. It is not always about skin color, sexual orientation, or your religion. Discrimination toward people with mental issues is very real and very ugly just like any other form of discrimination.

The original reason I didn't come out as bipolar was that I would never know if my patients would feel uncomfortable. Way back when I told my in-laws, my mother-in-law was so shocked it took her breath away. Acceptance and love eventually came, and we developed a trusting and loving relationship. The point is, even intelligent and worldly people can be profoundly fearful of someone with mental illness. I think they thought it was the end of the world for me.

We moved from Charlotte, North Carolina, to a little town of about 12,000 in Connecticut. I wanted to volunteer on the local ambulance squad. I retook the entire EMT course and scored the highest grade on the state test in the region. The course was given at the squad's classroom, so they got to know me pretty well. They said they were looking for more volunteers. I applied for an EMT position and waited for a reply. I knew they would have to do an extensive background and criminal history check. I hadn't gotten a traffic ticket in over thirty years, not even a parking ticket. I gave it a decent amount of time; I have had many background checks for the EMTs, paramedic school, and employment. After a month, I hadn't heard anything. After two months, I worried, and at the third month, I withdrew my application.

Before I applied, I had spoken to the president of the ambulance association, a fellow paramedic. I told him of my extensive education and experience. In my mind, there can be only one reason the board didn't gladly accept someone who had my credentials. Discrimination! They must have found out that I was bipolar. I don't know for sure, but I think for some reason, the powers that be did not want a mentally ill person in their midst. They were probably afraid I would embarrass their provincial rescue squad. It felt like my original rejection by the ambulance squad in my hometown. What do we have to do to prove ourselves? I know that I would never have been hired as an EMT or health aide years ago if I told my employer I was bipolar. How many lives do I have to save until someone wouldn't mind having me for a neighbor?

Sometimes when you tell people you have a mental illness, their behavior around you changes and you become somewhat of a stranger to them. I felt the invitations may stop, and they may avoid me. We had a very close friend who used to speak of someone she didn't even know was bipolar. She seemed to fear and avoid that person.

According to NAMI.org, one in five adults in America experience a mental illness. It seems to me almost everyone is either affected by mental illness or knows someone who is, often in their own family. Who are we fooling? We're discriminating against ourselves and family members.

There seems to be some progress and more acceptance of mental illness today than years ago, but we have a ways to go. Letting others know is a highly personal choice. Many with mental illness may say I was not brave enough to stand up for our cause. You're right, but I thought I could do more by proving what I could do, rather than shooting myself in the foot. My silence gave me many of the opportunities that I doubt I would have had otherwise. I can say I did as much or more than a "normal" person could do. Yes, we can make meaningful contributions if given the opportunity.

Stupid Overdose

We all know that adverse prescription drug-related events take an unacceptable number of lives. There are over a million medication errors in the US per year, many of which occur in the home. When you are dealing with a tenuous hold on reality and don't feel well, it's not surprising we make mistakes. Case in point, me.

I had been having a period of hypomania where I was having trouble getting to sleep. I was staying up until two or three in the morning and sometimes not going to bed at all. Most bipolars know how vital a regular life schedule is, especially when it comes to keeping a consistent schedule of adequate sleep. To help get some sleep, I was prescribed a sleeping pill. The prescription was way too strong, and the doctor reduced the prescription to half-strength pills. I always try not to overmedicate, so I took just half the low-dose tablets. After several weeks, I was still not sleeping well. One night I was having a particularly difficult time. This is where the stupid part comes in. Without calling my doctor, I adjusted the dose up a bit; being a hotshot paramedic who is well trained in administering drugs, that should be no problem. Wrong. I was sitting in my easy chair with the lights turned low, watching TV. I had a bunch of prescription bottles on my end table. I grabbed the wrong one. It was the original full-strength version of my sleeping pill. I had been taking what had amounted to one-quarter that strength. To put another nail in my coffin, I figured, why not take two. I still wasn't getting sleepy, so I took another.

At that point, I rapidly fell asleep in my chair. I was accidentally overdosing.

My wife came downstairs and told me to go to bed. I started up the stairs, and about halfway up, I passed out and fell backward over the rail to the floor about six feet below, landing on my head. I woke up with blood all over, and the ambulance crew asking me if I was okay. I told them I was but didn't win the argument about going to the hospital.

Diagnosis: scalp laceration, concussion with subdural hematomas (bleeding into the brain), traumatic brain injury. Two blood vessels in my brain were bleeding, and if they didn't stop, they would have to drill holes in my head to relieve the pressure on my brain. Like they say, I was lucky to be alive. I've seen people who broke their necks with a lot less trauma. It ended pretty well for me. I didn't die, wasn't paralyzed, and the brain bleeds stopped on their own. I did come away with brain injuries that would take a year to heal fully. My wife says that I was never quite the same after that, and my doctor says I walk a little funny, but I say I'm much more handsome and perky.

I'm Going to Kill Myself

We moved to North Carolina, to be close to our son. Things were going along pretty well. Nice house. Nice town. Nice job. Nice doctors. I was due for a depressive or manic episode. I don't worry about what might be coming as I couldn't handle that. I had been seeing orthopedic surgeons for over ten years, ever since my hips started hurting. The original X-rays showed osteoarthritis in both. The doctors said all the lifting and moving in my rescue career had done a job on me. They said they didn't want to put in new hips until I couldn't stand the pain anymore. I appreciate a surgeon who's not surgery happy, but after ten years, it got to be a bit much.

Surgery for the new hip was scheduled in two weeks. Great!

Not so great. In the two weeks before surgery, I really wimped out. Even though this was major surgery, it was a low-risk procedure. I worried excessively anyway and even imagined dying during the operation. I was getting very little sleep. On the day of surgery, I was not in good shape; I was exhausted. At the hospital, we went through admitting, the pre-surgery process, said goodbye to my wife, and was off to never-never land for a successful operation done by a highly skilled surgeon who had performed thousands of hip replacements.

When I woke up from the anesthesia, things were not as it was supposed to be. The clock on the wall of my room was sliding around the wall. Various spiders and reptiles were inhabiting my room, and I was talking to people who weren't there. Houston, we have a problem! Apparently, my regular psychiatric meds were not given. Instead, other drugs that were in my past history file were given by mistake. I had stopped taking those particular meds because of the severe side effects of mania. The combination of lack of sleep, anxiety, a predisposition of bipolar problems, and the wrong meds produced a basket case. The technical term for my post-op crazies was anesthesia delirium. This adventure of the mind is not uncommon with major surgery. Not a lot of comfort when the walls are alive. So I came away from surgery with delirium and an acute manic phase of bipolar. Here we go again.

I stayed overnight and was discharged into the care of my wife, a woman who probably should have left me years ago. I was not doing well at home. Luckily, I was in contact with my counselor and psychiatrist. I was a burden on my family again. This crap had been going on for years. It was getting old, and I was tired of it. How long would this latest setback last? I could hardly sleep because I had to stay in one position all night so as not to dislocate my new hip. I never realized how hard that would be. Would I ever get better, or would I stay crazy forever? I felt isolated, alone, and started dwelling on the worst-case scenario. For the first time in my life, I seriously thought of the benefits suicide would give me. Finally to be free of the relentless discouragement of a mind that's not right and to free others from the pain I caused them. I wanted to punish the brain that had dealt me this hand. I didn't have to put up with this anymore.

The best punishment for this out-of-control organ was to kill it. I was ready, willing, and able. I confided to my wife that I wanted to kill myself. I couldn't even get to see my doctor as I was not recovered enough from surgery, so my counselor started calling me on the phone, talking to me, and giving useful advice. In the million years I had been seeing counselors and psychiatrists, they never once called me at home. But now, on speakerphone, my shrink walked us through the medications and dosages he thought would help. The calls continued, and when I started coming out of the woods, they continued checking on me through texts. Say what you want about healthcare providers, but with my wife's support, they saved my life.

I had never come that close before. The takeaway is that I was lucky enough to have an observant support group in place, and they were caring enough to help me and follow through. Without my wife as my chief advocate, things might have been way different. I think if I had no such network, I still might have made it by talking to people and sharing how I felt. A family doctor, relative, friend, or acquaintance can make all the difference.

The fact that I survived gave me a new appreciation of life and the things I would have missed. Please consider what is left behind with suicide. The family and friends who know you have lost a loved one and are hurt deeply and permanently. It's not just you that you are killing but a part of them as well. There aren't many people who truly want to harm others. You end your personal pain, but those closest to you in life will continue to experience sadness and anger that will last forever.

You will see how fast things can change for the better if you give it more time. Look what happened to me. If I had killed myself, I wouldn't have become a fabulously wealthy author selling ten or twenty copies of this book.

Bipolar disorder can become so absolutely unbearable one in five of us kill ourselves.[1] Let me repeat. About one in five of us kill ourselves. This is twenty times higher than the national average for suicide and the worst outcome for all the mental illnesses. There has been a silent taboo that we have barely begun to talk about. I have been bipolar for over half a century. I have been educated and worked in the health field most of my life, but I have not heard these shocking facts until I was doing research for this book. This is something we don't talk about. It's not going away. It's getting worse. We have been silent for so very long. No more!

If you find yourself contemplating suicide, talk to someone.

National Suicide Prevention Lifeline

1-800-273-8255

Available twenty-four hours a day, seven days a week.

The Crooked Man

I was sitting in the waiting room of my doctor's office, having a nasty reaction to a medication and thinking why was I so unlucky to have to be taking this medicine and then suffering from its effects? Poor me. Into the room walks a tall stick of a man with a massive smile on his face. He was contorted and walked with a shuttering motion, consciously putting one foot in front of the other. None of the movements of his limbs matched the movements of the opposite limbs. It looked like different parts of his body were trying to go in different directions. His head was crooked. I had seen people with various degrees of infirmity, but this guy seemed to have everything. I couldn't help but stare. He looked right at me with the biggest, most genuine smile and a nod.

He actually made me feel good as he staggered past me and sat down, half in and half out of the chair. I eventually was called in to see the doctor, and my medication problem was solved. When I left, the young man was still there, spreading love around the room. Since that day, I never felt sorry for myself or my situation without thinking of him. I saw the power of love.

Little Boy

After mental illness, the horror and satisfaction of ambulance work, nagging fear of going insane and never coming back, relentless cycles of bipolar, failures, adventures, gifts of life, mistakes, and fears, I found myself on the sidewalk where a little boy should have met his death.

It was a recent Memorial Day. I wanted to see the last day of a World War I exhibition at the History Museum in downtown Raleigh. There was a ceremony about to get underway in a little park across the street. We went over to see, but it was going to be a while till it started, so we decided to go back to the museum. About twelve or fifteen people were crowded together waiting for the traffic light to change. We were standing where there was no curb, and the traffic was whizzing by us at an uncomfortably high speed. A little boy of about three or four broke away from his mother and jumped right into oncoming traffic. A white SUV was upon him. I took a step or two and hooked my arm around him and yanked him back to the curb. Astonishingly when I let him go, he headed right back into traffic. Again, my arm hooked around him. The traffic had not slowed and another car was almost on us hitting us with a cold rush of wind. My wife grabbed me and the boy, saving us both.

Now there would be no broken little boy, no shattered glass, no pain, no fear, no suffering, and no grief. Oblivious, he looked up at me with wide eyes as if to say "Why are you holding me?" I edged him over to his mother, who was starkly quiet. She finally said, "Thank you for saving my little boy's life." It sounds corny, but I replied, "It's what I do. I'm a paramedic."

Across the street on the steps of the museum, I cried for the little boy. I never cried for my patients, but at that moment, I wept for all of them. I had lived a life, but it all could have been replaced by that one moment. Even though I am no longer technically a professional paramedic, I can still make a difference. We all can.

There is a beginning, middle, and end of life. For sure, it is finite. We may not have much control of the beginning or end, but in the middle, we are very much alive. What you make of your allowed speck of time is mostly up to you, taking responsibility for yourself and how you interact with the world around you.

Everything we know comes from stardust. The earth, oceans, us. For some reason or maybe no reason at all, we are here together for a short time. Some of us are this way, and some of us are that way as we seek comfort and happiness. I believe we all want to be loved and that all of us want to love.

No matter what happens, I am happy to be here. This is the way it's supposed to be!

---

1. Goodwin FK, Jamison KR. *Manic-Depressive Illness*. New York: Oxford University Press; 1990.
   https://www.psychiatrictimes.com/view/suicide-attempts-and-completions-patients-bipolar-disorder

FINAL THOUGHTS

Accepted truths don't always turn out to be correct. Who's to say today's beliefs are right? The earth was once considered flat, then round, and now it's known that it's not exactly round either. What is accepted truth today may not be true in the future.

With advances in medicine and treatments, we are already controlling many of the downsides of bipolar disorder. New medications continue to be developed. Maybe it will even be possible to limit the confusion and suffering of bipolar disorder, allowing energy, creativity, innovation, and motivation to soar. Most employers would welcome higher productivity and forward thinking in their employees, not to mention that those with a little mania going on can be fun to be with.

In the not-so-distant future, will they call today's smartphone users Neanderthals? Call me crazy, but why not? Is the application of useful bipolar traits part of our human evolution? It's not far-fetched when you think of the advances in medicine.

There you have it. Over a half century of dealing with bipolar.

I guess, looking back at some of the horribly desperate times that life and mental illness presented, there have been a lot of ups and downs, but what else would you expect? It's bipolar disorder. It has lived up to its reputation of extremes. It was touch and go many times, and I'm still not sure the cruel black depression or the destructively tempting high of mania will not return, but I know if I follow my own advice, I can deal with it as it comes.

Even though normal periods between the ups and downs may not last as long as I like, I relish these good times in my relationships and work life. It's been wonderful meeting remarkable people with mental illness who were full of warmth, intelligence, and creativity. I had met my "California girl" and lived high in the Rocky mountains I loved. We were so glad we took the chance to have a baby so many years ago! We loved raising our son and watching T-ball, baseball, basketball, scouts, and everything else raising a child entailed, even including trips to the emergency room for asthma and stitches. We've seen the Sistine Chapel together, watched monkeys in the Costa Rican jungle, and almost drowned together scuba diving on a coral reef on Bonaire off the coast of Venezuela in the southern Caribbean. I treasure the family vacations at Mary's grandmother's cottage on Pelican Lake, Minnesota. Watching exquisite sunrises over the Atlantic at the North Carolina Outer Banks filled me with hope and a feeling of oneness with the everyone. No matter what, the sun will rise and fall for each of us.

I am happy to be here. You could say that at least life was rarely boring! I have made a difference in my everyday life, even after my paramedic career ended. I sincerely believe helping others is the fastest and most satisfying way to help yourself. I genuinely wish you love. I believe love can save us as individuals, and love can save us as a society. Live your life on your terms with proper treatment, support, and extraordinary effort by you.

You've got this! Take it and run with your bipolar rescue.

APPENDIX A: THINGS TO GET YOU THROUGH

This appendix has things I've learned to get me through difficult times and sometimes has helped me along with fun and motivation. I'm continuing to learn. It helps to have these ideas written down for reference because when you are in the middle of an episode, you can't remember half of what has helped in the past. I doubt if a lot of this is brand new to you. Besides, you have sense enough to know what works for you or to research what does work. Add your own ideas.

Tips

1. Obtain the correct diagnosis from a health care provider, preferably a psychiatrist. Accept your illness and work hard to stay well. It can be hard, but you are more resilient than you think.
2. Persevere! Staying well is hard work. There will be setbacks and it's hard when you're depressed or manic, but never give up. Don't be discouraged by relapses. They happen and you'll get through them. Be patient with yourself. You will heal and get better.

Know your healthy mind will come back; it will get
better.

3. When mood swings happen or if PTSD recurs, get
help sooner rather than later. The longer symptoms
last, the harder it is to bounce back.

4. Scrupulously take your meds! Consult your medical
professional before stopping. Never stop on your own.
Never.

5. Save money on your meds by checking with
pharmaceutical companies for discounts.

6. No recreational drugs; it's not recommended to drink
with most medications.

7. Keep a regular routine and consistent schedule. I have
found it is imperative for me.

8. Maintain good nutrition, low sugar/salt, and plenty of
water.

9. Regular exercise from increasing your activity around
the house, walking, biking, weights, yoga, or the gym
helps.

10. Learn about your illness so you can be aware of what
is happening.

11. Talk about and explain your illness to family and
friends. This book may help them start to
understand.

12. Learn from your past patterns of wellness and
sickness so you can copy or avoid them. Keep a
journal; it's easier that way to track ups and down as
well as triggers.

13. When you are feeling good, write something positive
and practical to help your depressed or manic self.
That's how I came up with this list.

14. Don't blame yourself for your illness. It's not your
fault.

15. Don't take life too seriously. Laugh and see humor

where you can. Laughing produces pleasant brain chemicals like dopamine.

16. Balance what you do. Moderation in all things.
17. Getting with nature can improve your mood and outlook.
18. A pet, plants, and flowers can do wonders.
19. Join a support group. Many providers see improvement in patients who go to support meetings. You will see you're far from being alone.
20. Enjoy the accomplishments of chores and obligations that you do.
21. Don't get behind in school, job, or tasks because it causes undo stress and makes it harder if you do run into a bipolar episode. You will be more prepared for what the future brings.
22. Keep learning because it fights boredom, provides focus, and helps you advance.
23. Try new things out of your comfort zone.
24. You may want to get involved in a social cause or volunteer project. There are few better feelings I get then when I'm helping somebody other than myself.
25. Live your life, take chances, and set realistic goals for the short and long term. Put yourself out there. You might make a contact for a job or meet a friend or someone special.
26. If there seems to be no fun or excitement where you are or in your current situation, read a book, magazine, watch movies or TV. The internet has limitless sources of fun. If you're not in the mood for media, get in a quiet place and let your imagination create a better day. As time passes, you can make those things real.
27. Make it a point to do something for yourself every day.

28. Listen or play music to relax, motivate, and realize your thoughts and feeling are shared by others.

Some of my favorites:

- "Gravity" by Sara Bareilles. For those who love even though it hurts sometimes. There is a music video on YouTube.
- "Blue" by Joni Mitchell. For those of us when we are depressed.
- "How to Save a Life" by The Fray. For all those who save lives in so many different ways. This is also on YouTube.

Relationships and Socialization

1. Understand that while bipolar, there is a tendency to be selfish or self-centered. Be considerate of others.
2. Ask loved ones for help but not for every little thing. Remember you are responsible for yourself as much as possible. When you help yourself when you can, your loved ones are more willing to help when you can't.
3. Avoid being too critical. At times it may be a sign of your illness. You don't want to damage your relationships.
4. Continue to love family and people in general. Love is powerful, feels good, and is generally returned to you.
5. Find others to share your spirituality with.
6. Love can hurt at times. We're all in the same boat.
7. Keep your word as a promise to do what you say. No half-truths. This is harder than it sounds when manic or depressed.
8. Be honest with yourself and family.

9. Listen to loved ones, friends, and health care providers. They may have good advice or can see problems before you are aware of them.
10. Avoid isolation; socialize with family, friends, neighbors, even the clerk at the store.
11. Avoid negative and destructive people.
12. A clean orderly living space can be a comfort and stabilizing factor. It gives you a feeling of pride and control.

Handling Mania

1. Don't make big decisions while manic or depressed, you're more likely to be wrong.
2. Do not do finances or make large purchases or gamble while manic or depressed, same reason.
3. You may want to ask a trusted family member or friend to handle bills and finances for you, especially if you're going into the hospital.
4. Maintaining a good credit rating, if possible, is good for the future.
5. Don't overdo socialization, but don't isolate.
6. Avoid risky and destructive behavior including hypersexuality.
7. Remember your physical, mental, and emotional capabilities before you act on almost anything. Avoid overextending.
8. Stay busy but relax. Deep breathing, meditation, yoga, tai chi, walking, enjoying nature can all help you relax.
9. If you find yourself in a group and getting more and more wound up, step away if only for a few minutes. This can help you reset to get through the situation. It's incredibly hard do when you are manic.

10. Very important to keep a regular daily routine and sleep schedule.
11. Listen more than you talk.

Handling Depression

1. Do at least one thing every day even if it is small. Start small; even small efforts can help you feel better. Get out of bed, take a shower, do the dishes, take a walk. You can then build on it. Understand that this can be tough when in the middle of depression.
2. Redirect feelings of despair, feelings of death, poor health, suffering, into a more constructive and positive internal conversation, such as "This too shall pass. I will come back and be myself. I am not a disappointment to myself but rather am living the best life I can."
3. Physical activity has been proven to help depression, sometimes as much as medication. Walking, running, exercise, the gym, dancing, less sitting and more moving around the house.
4. Help others. Pay it forward and volunteer. Helping others helps you get away from your own concerns, and your problems seem smaller. Doing things for others is a joy.
5. Socialize so you don't become isolated.
6. Do something big or small that makes you happier every day. The little things help. Try to have fun and enjoy even little things. Color, play with a pet, try a new recipe.
7. Don't wallow in your illness; it's your responsibility to get and stay well. It is okay for a while, and may at times be necessary, but don't stay there for long.
8. Try not to go through life in the "why me" self-pity

and sadness of blaming yourself and others for something that is just a part of you. This will happen from time to time, but try not to live there.

9. Accept that you are not perfect.
10. Remember you are not dying. Things may seem bleaker than they are.
11. Things will get better; they always have in the past. It may take longer than you think it should. Be patient.
12. Don't worry about what is out of your control.
13. It may be a good time to cut back on the news.
14. Share thoughts, needs, and wants.
15. If you feel like harming yourself or others, it's time to call the doctor, talk to family, friends, or go to the emergency room. There is usually a local suicide hotline and always a national hotline. You will be amazed at how much they care and how things will turn around for you.

National Suicide Prevention Lifeline
1-800-273-8255
Available twenty-four hours a day, seven days a week.

Good Sleep Hygiene

There are whole books written on this subject. What I have found useful are:

1. No caffeine before bed; no coffee, tea, or chocolate.
2. Go to bed and get up at the same time every night including weekends.
3. Do not do anything too stimulating before bed. No TV, social media, or other electronics.
4. If you can't sleep, get out of bed and do something boring like reading something that is uninteresting to

you and easy to put down, or some light cleaning. Boring stuff makes you sleepy.

5. Listen to music or meditate.
6. If you can't sleep, try not to look at the clock. It doesn't help.
7. Get up at the same time even if you didn't sleep, that way you'll probably sleep the next night.
8. A short nap in early afternoon is okay and may be helpful. Nothing too long or too close to evening or you may not sleep well that night.

Working with Health Care Providers

1. Seek out competent psychiatrists and counselors that you have rapport with by using doctor referrals, word of mouth, or internet referral sites.
2. I have found a combination of psychiatrists to manage symptoms and medication, and a counselor for talk therapy can work well.
3. You may want to get a second opinion.
4. Contact your health care professionals soon if symptoms start to show up, and keep your appointments.
5. Keep up with your counselor and other healthcare providers. Share your problems and concerns with them.
6. Video and telephone appointments may be available.
7. Be honest with your providers. Tell them what you expect and need, and ask questions.
8. Consider going to the hospital if your family, friends, and medical providers recommend it and it is necessary. Besides helping you, it can provide a respite for your family or caregiver. Private and state hospitals are doing a better job today than in the past.

Work

1. A job can provide income, socialization, pride, and insurance.
2. Work can improve quality of life. It can also increase stress, so strive for balance.
3. Consider a work-from-home job if you struggle with your work environment. The internet has opened many possibilities.
4. If finances allow, reduce your employment to part-time, which may reduce stress.
5. If you can't work, consider pursuing disability. You may be able to get disability through work benefits or from Federal Social Security disability benefits. Call Social Services in your county to see what other services are available.
6. State Rehabilitation Commissions can be a source of education and job training.
7. You may want to consider who and when you disclose your illness to. Everyone doesn't understand, and it could limit opportunities. On the flip side, if you decide to disclose, you may find an ally who can help and understand, but there is a risk.
8. It helps to have an understanding boss and flexible hours for when you don't feel well. You need to decide for yourself about informing your employer about your condition. There is still discrimination.
9. Build up vacation and sick time so you'll have time off available when the bad days arrive.
10. Prepare ahead of expected hard times so you have a cushion of savings.
11. Specialize and excel at your chosen field. The respect and confidence you gain is rewarding and builds self-esteem.

APPENDIX B: TRIGGERS

Be aware of triggers that can lead to either depression or mania. Triggers and warning signs can vary by person, so it helps to pay attention to what happened right before an episode. Become familiar with your triggers, and be on guard for possible warning signs when they happen. You may want to keep a journal to record your thoughts, stress, big events, medication, and sleep. You will probably see patterns show up.

1. Any stressful situation or major life event can be a trigger.
2. New, different, or changed relationships.
3. Death or illness of a loved one.
4. Sometimes even good events can trigger a hypomanic or depressive episode. A vacation, job promotion, holidays, new baby. Any of these can initiate a dangerous cycle.
5. Financial change.
6. Physical, sexual, or psychological abuse.
7. Being a victim of discrimination or crime.
8. Drug or alcohol abuse.

9. Overstimulation or excitement.
10. Major changes in routine / going off regular schedule.
11. Being around too many people. Being too socially active. This varies by person. Some people are naturally more social.
12. Traveling across many time zones.
13. Seasonal mood swing patterns. Spring and summer seem to set some of us off, while fall and winter affect others.
14. Lack of sleep.
15. Working too many hours.
16. Stopping meds or an error in medication. Always double check your prescriptions before taking them.
17. Hormonal changes, especially in women.
18. Poor nutrition; too much sugar or caffeine.
19. High temperature can trigger mania.

APPENDIX C: WARNING SIGNS

Everyone has their ups and downs, and it can be difficult to know the difference between a warning of mania or depression verses a normal happiness or sadness. Keeping a log or journal and listening to people close to you can help you learn and recognize your own warning signs.

Mania Warning Signs

1. Change in sleep patterns, sleeping less, insomnia.
2. Lower concentration, doing many things at once, more than normal, often inefficiently.
3. Things are "too beautiful" or "too good."
4. Increased appetite; food tastes great.
5. Loss of appetite; too busy to eat.
6. Can't relax; have to be on the go all the time.
7. Hard to "behave" in social situations.
8. Fast staccato speech. Talking too much. Doing most of the talking.
9. Joking around too much. Not concerned about the audience.

10. Not listening. Interrupting everyone.
11. Feeling self-important.
12. Critical and incessant comments.
13. Yelling at the television.
14. Racing thoughts.
15. Spending beyond your means or more than usual.
16. Unrealistic confidence.
17. Increased sexuality.
18. Oversensitive to stimuli: noises are louder, colors are brighter, smells are stronger.
19. Obsessing; little things and passions are amplified sometimes at the expense of getting other things done.
20. On a soapbox; feeling obligated to correct / train people.
21. Singing all the time.
22. Making lists upon lists upon lists.
23. Confusion; misplacing keys, money, and documents.
24. Driving faster or more carelessly.
25. Becoming too selfish or self-centered.
26. Increased impatience.

Depression Warning Signs

1. Change in sleep patterns, sleeping too much or too little.
2. Trouble getting out of bed.
3. Can't accomplish anything. Not wanting to try.
4. Cranky.
5. Not taking care of yourself; poor hygiene, poor diet.
6. Not being able to concentrate and focus.
7. Obsessing: little things and passions are amplified sometimes at the expense of getting other things done.

8. Forgetting scheduled appointments.
9. Just not caring about anything.
10. Feelings of hopelessness, thoughts of suicide.

Suicide is preventable. If you feel like harming yourself, it's time to call the doctor, talk to family, friends or go to the emergency room. There is usually a local suicide hotline and always a national hotline. You will be amazed at how much they care and how things will turn around for you.

National Suicide Prevention Lifeline
1-800-273-8255
Available twenty-four hours a day, seven days a week.

Made in the USA
Columbia, SC
26 September 2020